YOU'RE AMAZING™

AMAZING

A MESSAGE OF **HOPE** THAT WILL CHANGE YOUR LIFE FOREVER

JUSTIN FATICA

ISBN: 978-1-929266-14-2 (softcover)

Design by Madeline Harris

Unless otherwise noted, Scripture passages have been taken from the *Revised
Standard Version, Catholic Edition.* Copyright 1946, 1952, 1971 by the Division of
Christian Education of the National Council of Churches of Christ in the USA.
Used by permission. All rights reserved.

Quotes are taken from the English translation of the *Catechism of the Catholic
Church* for the United States of America (indicated as *CCC*), 2nd ed. Copyright
1997 by United States Catholic Conference—Libreria Editrice Vaticana.

Library of Congress Cataloging-in-Publication Data
Names: Fatica, Justin, author.
Title: You're amazing : a message of hope that will change
your life forever / Justin Fatica.
Description: North Palm Beach, Florida : Beacon Publishing, 2017.
Identifiers: LCCN 2017002000| ISBN 9781929266142 (pbk. : alk. paper) |
ISBN 9781929266159 (e-book) | ISBN 9781929266821 (audiobook)
Subjects: LCSH: Christian life. | Enthusiasm--Religious aspects--Christianity.
Classification: LCC BV4501.3 .F377 2017 |
DDC 248.4--dc23

Dynamic Catholic® and Be Bold. Be Catholic.® and The Best Version of
Yourself® are registered trademarks of The Dynamic Catholic Institute.

For more information on this title or other books and CDs available through
the Dynamic Catholic Book Program, please visit www.DynamicCatholic.com.

The Dynamic Catholic Institute
5081 Olympic Blvd • Erlanger • Kentucky • 41018
Phone: 1–859–980–7900
Email: info@DynamicCatholic.com

10   9   8   7   6   5   4   3

Printed in the United States of America

TABLE OF CONTENTS

IV. BE HUMBLE

V. BE ENCOURAGING

ACKNOWLEDGMENTS

FOREWORD

One of the earliest lessons I learned from my parents is the importance of being passionate in life. For my mother and father, passion did not mean simply having strong emotions about something or someone. Rather, passion was the power that flowed from the presence of the Holy Spirit in our lives, giving us a share in the same spiritual fire that came upon the heads of the Apostles at Pentecost. Such passion can empower us to become faithful disciples of Christ, fulfill our duties each day with generosity, courageously love those around us, and persevere before whatever challenges we may face. Without such passion, life can easily become mediocre, routine, and boring.

We can all recognize the difference between a person who is passionate about his or her faith and one who is not. There is a joy that comes from passionate believers that is both inviting and infectious. Believers who are on fire with God's grace build bridges of understanding between people, show compassion for those who are hurting, and bring hope to those in despair.

The questions that you and I must ask ourselves are: How passionate are we about the life God has given us? Do we want to be on fire with love for God and our neighbor?

If you answer yes to any of these questions, this book, *You're Amazing: A Message of Hope That Will Change Your Life Forever*, is all about inviting the fire of the Holy Spirit into your life. It is a powerful spiritual tool for anyone who wishes to live joyfully and effectively. In a world where we are given many reasons to doubt whether we are loveable or loved and are tempted to fall into isolation, fear, and indifference, Justin outlines a practical and compelling spiritual itinerary that is nothing short of revolutionary. I am confident that if you read this book, you will leave behind any desire to live a mediocre or routine life. In its place, you will be invited to live with real meaning and passion.

Most Reverend Frank J. Caggiano
Episcopal Advisor, Hard as Nails

PART I
Be Real

GET NAKED

Whoever walks in integrity will be delivered, but he who is perverse in his ways will fall into a pit.

—*Proverbs 28:18*

How do you define being "real"? What is a real person? The way I look at it, a real person is always genuine and authentic, and is all around a person of integrity—he is who he is, no matter where he is. This person has nothing to hide, nothing to fear, and nothing to lose. A real person is at peace and remains joyful no matter what life's circumstances bring. As the old hymn exclaims, "No storm can shake my inmost calm while to that refuge clinging, since Christ is Lord of Heaven and earth how can I keep from singing?" A real person knows that as long as she is real about who she is, who God is, and how that relationship is growing, nothing can shake her. That is reason for hope; that is a recipe for fulfillment.

But does the idea of such "realness" seem impossible or intimidating to you? Many of us balk at it in today's world, because we have an image we still feel the need to cling to. Others of us may be on board (hey, it kind of sounds like a trendy cleanse), only to lose our nerve when anxiety sets in. Perhaps we will accidentally become too real. It is natural to resist feeling vulnerable, open to societal judgment, and permanently out of one's comfort zone—essentially, being spiritually and emotionally naked.

Well, here is the naked truth: I discovered that if a person decides to hand his or her life over to God—and I mean completely—then that person is an example of what it means to be real. I don't know if you have made that decision, but if you have, you have a good shot at living an amazing life, because being real is step one. As we go through these five life-changing steps, we will discover just how to hand our lives over to God. But don't make your decision just yet—start by being real; it can't kill you!

"Realness" in front of God is the ultimate confidence. There is no shame in nakedness when we are naked in front of our Creator—he knows us better than we know ourselves anyway. We never have to be afraid when we allow God to take charge. He is our rock: "Be a rock of refuge for me, a strong fortress to save me! Yes, you are my rock and my fortress; for your name's sake lead me and guide me" (Psalm 31:2–3). Here's how being real helped some of my friends become fully confident in who they are and compassionate toward others.

TODD'S STORY

In our apostolate, Hard as Nails, we are on a mission to awaken the world to the power of God's love. During one of our events I met a young man named Todd. I was speaking at a family conference in 2010, and my first impression of him was that he just seemed to have it all together. People enjoyed spending time with Todd; they gravitated toward his magnetic personality. He was a straight-A student who had never taken drugs or engaged in underage drinking or had sex before marriage. He came from a wonderful, loving family. Here's the thing, though: Families and kids perceived as perfect and wonderful are not exempt from suffering.

During my talk that day, I asked a simple question: "Would anyone like to share their story?" Todd was the very last person to step up to the mic. I had a feeling he had been waiting for the perfect opportunity to be real about the challenges he had been facing. This was it.

When he got up in front of the group, Todd shared that he habitually cut himself—a devastating addiction many teens succumb to. He opened up his beautiful heart and talked about the anxiety he faced on a daily basis. With some timidity, yet with powerful conviction, Todd told the crowd that he needed God to help him overcome his addiction to cutting; he knew he couldn't do it on his own. Because he was willing to be real in admitting his need for God, Todd had been set free and found a deeper sense of purpose in his life that day.

RANDY'S TURN

"I'm Randy. Thanks for helping my son," Todd's father said later that day, offering me a firm handshake. With tears in his kind eyes, he expressed his deep appreciation for my helping Todd speak up about his pain. Having had no idea what Todd was going through, Randy experienced real angst after hearing his son's poignant confession.

As I got to know Randy at that weeklong conference, I asked him what challenges he was facing in life. He deflected, "Oh, you know, my son . . . I just want to help my son." I wanted to know what his personal challenges were, not what his son was facing—I already knew about that. Randy and I became friends that week, and he made a commitment to be real—not only with his family and those around him, but first and foremost with himself.

I kept in touch with Todd, and he shared with me that he was going through so much more than he had initially let on. He was cutting more than just his wrists. He was mutilating his legs too. His cutting had really become a severe addiction. The details he shared with me were just gruesome.

I encouraged him to share these intimacies with his parents. After some pushback he agreed, and he ended up talking with his mom and dad for more than forty-five minutes about the specific challenges he was facing. Persistence paid off—after a little extra prodding and digging, Todd was willing to be totally honest about his addiction, and thankfully his parents listened with their whole hearts. Although it was a tough conversation, it was the beginning of a new chapter for Todd and his parents.

You see, being real doesn't mean taking the easy path; instead, it often means taking a very difficult one. But it is the outcome of going through the discomfort and vulnerability of being real that makes us fulfilled. Being real was the beginning of Todd's and Randy's healing, wholeness, and freedom, and it can be the beginning for you too.

NO FILTER

It's one thing to be real with yourself, but to be real with others is an equally important component. Sharing your personal story, your suffering, your battles, your humanness, however ugly or embarrassing you think they are, is what enables you to advance ever closer toward a life of peace with yourself, others, and God.

Being this level of real isn't easy today; our world sometimes seems like one grand masquerade party. Everyone's photos are filtered to gain more likes on Instagram; males and females alike go so far as to edit images of themselves with Photoshop or whatever the latest trend is until they are nearly unrecognizable.

You see it everywhere you turn: politicians, celebrities, cliques at school or work. We are insecure and more self-involved than ever. Maybe we aren't intentionally hiding our brokenness, but we are flaunting our assets in order to garner attention, which is equally fraudulent on the "levels of fakeness" spectrum. We dance the dance because we want to build a following—a fan base centered around us. We want to be adored. We want to be celebrated. Whether or not we realize it, what we want is artificial gratification, which will only leave us empty in the end. Isn't it sad that many of us have been told that our worth and beauty are dependent on the way we portray ourselves to the (cyber) world? Isn't it a shame that we think we need add-ons and filters so that others will love us? But if we want to be content with who we are, we can't give in to the false affirmations offered on social media when we flaunt our exterior life. We need to be ourselves inside and out if we want to be fulfilled and satisfied with our lives.

The fakeness at this point has become so prevalent. For those of us who choose to be real and transparent, we've got our work cut out for us, but don't let your spirit be dampened by the overwhelming odds. I challenge you to take off your own masks and get "naked." If you are real with others, they are more likely to let you in, and if you pursue them with authentic love and keep digging deeper, they might even ask you to help them discard their masks.

QUOTE TO REMEMBER: "Your time is limited, so don't waste it living someone else's life." —Steve Jobs

TIME FOR GOD: Get a notebook or a journal or open the notes app on your phone. Ask God to help you gain deeper fulfillment by revealing to you the areas in your life where you need to "get naked." Make a list of three things you want to get real about, and pray for God to give you the grace and strength to confront these areas.

MAKE IT COUNT: Consider finding a mentor or spiritual director you can meet with regularly. Read this book and share with him or her your experiences as you walk through it together. If you cannot find a mentor or spiritual director, find a companion to walk through it with you. Amazing things will happen when you go two by two.

KID AT HEART

Whoever humbles himself like this child, he is the greatest in the kingdom of heaven.

—Matthew 18:4

BE A KID AGAIN

When you were a little kid, you could make a mistake, get back up, brush yourself off, and start over. When you were young, you could disappoint someone and not be ashamed when that person held you accountable—you might have just been ticked off for twenty minutes or so. When you were a child, you might have felt angry in the heat of the moment, but after your nap, you soon forgot about whatever had bothered you. When you were a kid, you could do something embarrassing without holding on to shame for years.

But often, as we get older, we begin to hold grudges: against our families, our friends, and even our past selves. We get upset over people's reactions and refuse to let those feelings go. Many times it takes years to finally get over an injustice or a betrayal, instead of just minutes. We need to get our "kid hearts" back so we can experience that freedom we once had to let God handle our difficulties.

CANNONBALL!

When we were kids we would jump into a pool without thinking twice. We would tear off our shirts, tie our bathing suits, and cannonball into the freezing cold water, envisioning in our imaginative little brains a splash the size of a four-hundred-pound man's. It was freeing, and boy was it was fun! We would swim for hours. We would never get tired. Our friends would enjoy themselves and it seemed as though there was never anything wrong in the world—except for when we splashed those nice old ladies at the pool (but come on—was that really so wrong?). What a great life! But what happened to those kids? When did we lose those carefree and excitable little hearts?

Fast-forward—now we take *forever* to get in the water. If it's cold, we might sit there until kingdom come just hoping no one is going to pressure us to get in. And this is one of our obstacles to living an amazing life. We weigh our options so much that fear and the trepidation at what might happens paralyzes us. We miss opportunities because we are sitting around waiting for other people to give us permission to be that kid again. We wait for people to believe in us, when in reality we already are *amazing*! By the power of our baptismal calling, we are truly a gift, and the way we live our life is how we show the world who we are and who our Father is. Being a kid at heart means being ready to take on this world with the power that dwells within us. Let that little kid out again—you won't regret it.

QUOTE TO REMEMBER: "When I became a man I put away childish things, including the fear of childishness and the desire to be very grown up." —C. S. Lewis

TIME FOR GOD: Ask God to prepare you to let go of all the things holding you back from being a kid again. Write in your journal three things that are holding you back.

MAKE IT COUNT: Go out and do something that you used to love doing as a kid (swimming, throwing rocks, shooting some hoops, getting ice cream, etc.). Fulfillment happens when you love life. People are inspired by someone who loves his or her life and is carefree like a kid.

KEEP IT SIMPLE

And he said to him, "You shall love the Lord your God
with all your heart, and with all your soul, and with all
your mind. This is the great and first commandment.
And a second is like it, You shall love
your neighbor as yourself."

—*Matthew 22:37–39*

THOU SHALL NOT BE DRAMATIC

I'll never understand how so many people are able to keep up with those Kardashians! (Not that I have any desire to try to, I might add.) Keeping up with every detail of anyone's life is just too complicated. If we try to, we'll wear ourselves out. Let's opt for simplicity instead. Simplicity is crucial to a life of fulfillment. We need to love people simply and truthfully. Practically speaking, all we need to do is periodically ask ourselves, "Am I keeping things simple?" When we get caught up in drama, it only complicates things. Here are some phrases that can lead to "drama for your mama," as I like to say. If these are running through your head, you need to simplify your life by getting rid of some drama:

"Does she like me?"

"He is so much better at _____ than I am."

"Did you hear what _____ did?"

"She's so mean to me, but I'm *always* nice to her."

"I loved him and he hurt me. What a _____ !"

I think you get the point. Being caught up in other people's lives and making comparisons is unnecessary drama. In this life there will always be a parade of drama surrounding you and the people you know. But do your best to steer clear of it and your life will begin to become simple again. Instead of comparing yourself to others, reflect inwardly—love those who hurt you and protect those who are vulnerable to being hurt by others.

The more we overthink, the more we overanalyze, the more we overextend our resources into things that aren't life giving, the less simple our life becomes. Life becomes more complicated and our relationships become more confusing and self-seeking. These experiences become unbearable.

Stay away from drama in your romantic relationships, too. It gets complicated when you get caught up in a relationship that won't last or eventually lead to marriage. If you truly love that person, then you will stop focusing on defining the relationship and start focusing on what is best for him or her and for yourself. If you are married, don't think about what you wish your spouse would be. Concentrate on seeing the good in him or her and find ways for your spouse to be the-best-version-of-himself or -herself. The same is true with your children. "No one has greater love than this, to lay down one's life for one's friends" (John 15:13). Love is simple. Look for what is best for others, and you will love with a sacrificial love like Christ.

FOCUS ON WHAT MATTERS

Life is too short to worry about things that don't matter. We stress ourselves out about little things that mean nothing. People spend too much time thinking about their results on a Facebook test and not enough time thinking about how they can get out there and love the people around them. Last year I took a Facebook challenge that promised to measure my "lovability." My wife, Mary, did this with me—and of course, she was 100 percent lovable. Mary said, "Your turn, Justin!" So I, confident man that I am, answered the questions and waited for my results. The computer buffered for a while, and I started to get kind of nervous. I told my wife, "Watch, I'll probably be only 5 percent lovable." We both laughed, thinking I'd at least do better than that! Finally the arrow circled around and came back with my score: 1 percent lovable. Ha! You see, God even loves the guy the Internet deems unlovable! The thing that makes me amazing is that I was loved when I was unlovable.

💡 **QUOTE TO REMEMBER:** "If you can't explain it to a six-year-old, you don't understand it yourself." —Albert Einstein

✝ **TIME FOR GOD:** Pray the Our Father until you get to the words "Thy will be done." Then repeat that phrase five times before moving on to the rest of the prayer. The Our Father is a simple prayer that will help you get back to the basics.

> *Our Father, Who art in heaven,*
> *hallowed be Thy Name;*
> *Thy kingdom come,*
> *Thy will be done (x 5),*
> *on earth as it is in heaven.*
> *Give us this day our daily bread,*
> *and forgive us our trespasses,*
> *as we forgive those who trespass against us;*
> *and lead us not into temptation,*
> *but deliver us from evil.*
> *Amen.*

◎ **MAKE IT COUNT:** Make a commitment to text one person who you know needs a boost in his or her life. Let this person know you care by making a constant effort to share encouragement with a compassionate and spiritually validating text daily for one week.

SET GOOD PRIORITIES

Seek first his kingdom and his righteousness, and all things shall be yours as well.

—Matthew 6:33

In order to feel fulfilled, we need to get our life in the right order according to what really matters. When we put things first that shouldn't be first, we lose our peace. There is an order to the way things work in this world, and we will find our fulfillment when we keep our lives prioritized. Just look at how the sun rises and sets each day—imagine how thrown off we would be if the sun came up a few hours late one day! When you get the following four priorities straight, you won't believe what a difference it will make in your life.

PRIORITY 1: FAITH

Many people say to me, "I want to be like you." I tell them,

"You just be you, and be like Jesus, because he will never let you down." In his book *Rediscover Catholicism*, Matthew Kelly talks about being the-best-version-of-ourselves, and I think he would agree that we also need to be the most *real* versions of ourselves. The way to do this is to put your trust first and foremost in God, not in others. Others may lead you astray, regardless of their intentions. God knows best; you'll never go wrong by trusting him. Who will protect you in the midst of all adversity? God will. Who will provide shelter during the storm? God will. Who knows what's best for your kids, your wife, your friends? God does.

People are watching the way you live your life, and when you live a life of faith it inspires those who are feeling hopeless. Without faith you will disappoint those who are observing you. Whether you're aware of it or not, your social media followers see what you're doing. Whether you like it or not, your name has a brand attached to it. Do you want your name to inspire faith in others or disappointment? Do you put God first over making money and over your own desires, good or evil? Is God your number one priority? Your relationship with him must come first, not your career, not your parish involvement, not even the good you do for the poor. You want to make sure to maintain enough personal time with God first and foremost, so you can take care of what he's entrusted to you. Do you think you know what is best for you, or do you believe that God, the one who created you, knows even better? God will take care of you, but you need to seek him first and ask for his guidance in all that you do.

Give God the best, most real version of yourself and I promise you that he will raise your life to new heights. You will achieve greatness. Deep down we all desire greatness, and it comes only from putting faith first and admitting that we need our heavenly Father to take care of us. Take away all the fancy words and prayers, all the aesthetically pleasing masks, and get real with God. Admit that you've done wrong. Admit that you need him to guide you. God loves you just as much when you feel dirty and broken as when you're feeling on top of the world. He loves you when you are on your knees begging for help, because he lifts up the weak. Put faith first—it's those who pray and spend time with God who are the most real.

PRIORITY 2: FAMILY

When a close friend of mine attempted suicide, I was devastated. I wondered how I could have spent so much time with this friend without ever realizing that he wanted to give up on life. I took it personally. I couldn't sleep. I couldn't even pray because I blamed myself for what he had done. That next morning, I walked into my dining room and saw that my six-year-old daughter (whom I consider one of my spiritual directors and my number one "cheerleader") had written me more than twenty little notes. I cried as I read, "I love you"; "You mean so much to me"; "I love you this much" (with a drawing of a little person stretching out her arms); "You are amazing"; "Thank you for loving me"; and "I love you, Dad!" What did this tell me? The daughter God gave me is absolutely the perfect daughter for me—and she encouraged me at just the right time that day.

My family isn't perfect, but it is perfect *for me*. God created my family, each person in it, to be my domestic church. It's my job to love my family. It's also my job to let them love me. When my daughter is old enough, I'll tell her about my friend who tried to end his life and how grateful I am for her and those amazing notes she wrote at that time in my life. My family is my second priority.

When I ask young people what their greatest challenges are, they often respond, "I just want my father's love, my mother's encouragement, my sister's or brother's kindness, my friends' compassion and understanding, or my mentor's spiritual direction, exhortation, wisdom, and guidance." Our youth and young adults are looking for fulfillment. (If you are older, remember, only God is old—we are all just his little kids.) We have that opportunity to take part in a fulfilling life through our families.

FAMILY MISSION

Do you have a mission statement for your family? In 2008 my wife and I decided to write one for ours when we went to a Benedictine abbey one weekend for a retreat. We prayed, we reflected and discussed, and this is what we came up with: "To be great, to love Jesus first, and to love others no matter what."

When my son Joseph turned four, I started to teach him this phrase so that he would know the mission of our family. One day I was working out downstairs in our basement weight room. Joseph was wandering up and down the stairs, just wanting to be around me. I asked him from my weight bench, "What is our family mission statement?" I was hoping he would finally remember it. He mumbled, "To be graaaaateful."

Immediately I said, "Exactly, son!"

Without even knowing it, my son changed the word in our mission statement from *great* to *grateful*. I thought, *Yes, it's better to be grateful than great*. My wife agreed, and from that day forward it became part of our new mission statement. I learned that day with Joseph—just as I did when my daughter wrote me those simple notes during one of the toughest times of my friend's life—that we need our whole family. God gave them to us for a reason. Together we help each other make God our first priority.

Do you have a daily family prayer time? If not, could you start with a weekly one? My family prays the Rosary together every day. Sometimes there are only three of us at home. Sometimes it's all six of us. No matter what, we all know that sometime during the day, usually after dinner, our family members have each other's backs through prayer.

I gave a talk this year, and it wasn't flowing well for some reason. I took a break while one of our team members shared his story. As I stepped off the stage, I got a text from my wife that read, "We miss you. We love you, and we all understand you being gone. We are praying for you." After I got that text, the floodgates of power opened up and the Holy Spirit started moving. It was my family that made it happen. Team Fatica is of one heart and one mind.

Our families can help us to love God better and win more souls for Jesus. We were created to help each other get to heaven, and what better way to do this than as a family?

PRIORITY 3: FRUITFULNESS

If you died today, how many people would be on their way

to heaven because of you? My daughter often tells me, "Dad, I can't wait to go to heaven." (I always think to myself, *Wait a minute . . . I'm going first. God, please don't let her or any of my family members die first*.) She continues, "Daddy, I can't wait to go to heaven because I'll get to meet all the people you helped to get there." The first time she said this to me, I was blown away by my daughter's heart and simplicity, but also by the depth of wisdom she has about life. The way we live our life should bear fruit in the lives of others. If after we die, we have not changed one life, then was our life important?

Our whole goal in life should be helping others know God and get to heaven. If we really believe that the way to a life of fulfillment is through a relationship with God, then we should do our very best to help others get to heaven to be with him for all eternity. Life is short; as my father always said, "We are just a speck on this earth." What do we have to lose? We might not see the fruit of our lives here on earth, but we will see it in heaven. What kind of a legacy do you want to leave behind for your family—one that is focused on your own accomplishments and desires or one that is focused on what is best for others? What is best for others—faith and a relationship with God—should be our focus. If you want to make the most of life and be fulfilled, your life should inspire others to live for God too.

PRIORITY 4: FUN

Have *fun*. St. Don Bosco said it best: "Enjoy your life; just do not sin." Seeing you having fun is what gives others the impetus to look at themselves more deeply and question whether they enjoy their lives as much as we enjoy ours. But when people see Christians being so rigid that they don't seem to be enjoying their lives, the natural reaction is, "Why would I want that?" If people saw that Christians have truly fulfilling lives, they'd be *flocking* to the baptismal fonts!

We can have fun working out, riding roller coasters, hanging out with family, playing games, and so on. We can find so many ways to make our lives an adventure—but with a purpose. Often people see Christians living boring lives full of dreary days and burdensome checklists. Pope Francis said, "One of the more serious temptations which stifles boldness and zeal is a defeatism which turns us into querulous and disillusioned pessimists, 'sourpusses'" (*Evangelii Gaudium*, 85). But if we are really living a life for Christ, then we'd better be having a good time—because if you're doing it right, it's a wild adventure!

When someone who doesn't have a relationship with God sees Christians actually having fun, all sorts of preconceived notions are suddenly flipped on their heads. We bring people to Christ through our joy more than through anything else. St. Teresa of Calcutta said, "Joy is a net of love in which you can catch souls."

This sums up the four priorities in one sentence: With the help of your family, put God first, change the lives of those around you, and have fun doing it. It's as simple as that!

QUOTE TO REMEMBER: "I shall do everything for heaven, my true home." —St. Bernadette Soubirous

TIME FOR GOD: Journal about the priorities in your life. Write down the ways you want to grow in your faith, the ways you want to help your family become closer, how you want to make a difference in other people's lives, and ways you hope to have more fun. Set goals and come back to them after reading this book.

MAKE IT COUNT: Every week, every month, and every quarter write out something on your calendar that you are looking forward to doing with someone you love (for example, date night, a family trip, a retreat, or a camping or hiking trip). Fulfillment comes not from achieving results at work, but from enjoying time with those we love and who love us.

CELEBRATE YOUR WEAKNESSES

*"If I must boast, I will boast of the things
that show my weakness."*

—2 Corinthians 11:30

At a lunch meeting in Skaneateles, New York, I was introduced to *New York Times* best-selling author Ken Blanchard, who has since become my good friend and mentor. I had hoped we could help each other. Upon meeting me, he asked what my mission was. I said, "To be rejected. What's yours?"

Honestly, at that point in my life, the only noble thing I had ever achieved that I could share with this stranger was that I had been rejected for the sake of the Gospel. I met him at a time in our mission when many people—even a few of my friends— were denying that they worked with me. Unless they were broken (like I am), people didn't really want to hear the Gospel from our mission. They wanted the clean, conventional, tidy message that everything was going to run smoothly. Even at a young age, I knew that a clean-cut message is not reality. Being real means being messy sometimes, and rejection is a reality in everyone's life.

"Interesting," Ken said. He asked about my budget for the year. I told him. He said, "No, not the quarter; I want to know for the whole year."

I said, "Ken, ninety-six thousand . . . that is the whole year." At this point I thought, *Am I just wasting his time? I probably will never see him again.* But I decided to boast of my weakness again. I said to him, "You have to understand who you are meeting with. I got an 820 on my SATs—that was the math plus the verbal!"

He laughed heartily and said, "You beat me by forty!"

I looked up in awe. I thought to myself, *Wow! A great businessman is boasting of his weaknesses too. No way! This is so exciting.* Even if I never got to hang out with him again, I at least knew I could make a difference for Jesus Christ, because Ken had.

He continued to share what the world might look at as weaknesses. He opened up to me about how hard it was for him when he experienced rejection for bringing the Gospel to the world. He also told me how hard it was when he lost his house in a fire, but that God worked a miracle when Ken prayed, "God, houses are burning down in our neighborhood—you can take mine, but please do not take my son's." Ken's house did burn down, but his son's was one of the few that remained intact. For

Ken the hardest thing was losing the pictures, the gifts, and the memories of those he loved, but the whole experience taught him to get excited about the things that really matter because life is short.

During that conversation Ken gave me one of my favorite lines, one I use at many of my talks across the world: "Life is like a roll of toilet paper. In the beginning, you think you have a lot. But in the end, you realize you don't have much left!"

Life is too short to take ourselves too seriously. Rather than getting discouraged by our weaknesses, we can truly get excited about them because we know that it gives God the opportunity to come through for us.

💡 **QUOTE TO REMEMBER:** "Don't argue for other people's weaknesses. Don't argue for your own. When you make a mistake admit it, correct it, and learn from it— immediately." —Stephen R. Covey

✝ **TIME FOR GOD:** Journal about your weaknesses today when you spend time in prayer. Ask God to show you how he can make them into strengths.

🎯 **MAKE IT COUNT:** The next time your weaknesses get the best of you, get excited about your mistakes and thank God for his strength. Fulfillment happens when we fall forward, not backward.

LET GOD FIGHT YOUR BATTLES

"Come to me, all you who labor and are burdened, and I will give you rest."

—*Matthew 11:28*

LET GO AND LET GOD

These days there seems to be a surplus of devastating events on the evening news, in newspapers, and on the Internet. Suicide, rape, abuse, addiction, terrorist attacks, murders—no economic bracket or geographic location is exempt. Abortion is widely perceived as normal, and if you disagree with this you're labeled a bigot. Morality is a personal thing. When you take a stand, you'll likely be considered intolerant and judgmental. If you don't take a stand, you'll be praised for being accepting.

We need to understand that just because we disagree with someone, it doesn't mean we are hateful. If we disagree with someone and are still able to love that person, that is letting go and letting God be in control. It's hard to know what to do when there seem to be so many problems in the world, but it is only when we let go that we recognize that God is the one in control—we are not. I hate rape, suicide, abortion, wars, and terrorist attacks, but I can still love like Jesus. Jesus came into this world to embrace its pain and suffering and heal it with truth and joy.

Letting go and letting God handle your difficulties is hard. I remember a tough time when I was displaced by a school where I had served for many years. I still miss that community so much; I served there with all my heart and had a huge vision for what we could have accomplished. But I had to let go of my own plans and let God be in control. Then another time I faced rejection from a girl I really loved. I had to let go and let God handle the rejection. Now, after more than ten years, I can see clearly how each rejection made me a more loving, faithful, and hopeful person.

The challenges I've faced have made me the man I am today and the challenges you're facing now will make you the man or woman you'll be ten years from now. When we're obedient in the face of injustice, patient with ourselves and others when we make mistakes, and confident that God will come through when things just don't make sense, we learn to recognize that God is in control and we can count on him to help us overcome every obstacle. He will never give us anything we can't handle.

REJECTION WILL BEAR FRUIT

My own rejections have usually happened because of pride, but they came during times when I needed to grow. Rejection is a great gift and will bear much fruit if handled properly. We have to learn to let God fight our battles. When he is fighting for us, we will gain the confidence we need to not be afraid of these battles. We will be honest enough to admit when we've been hurt and humble enough to seek direction, even if the results sting. Remember, Jesus knows what it feels like to be rejected.

John 12:24 says, "Amen, amen, I say to you, unless a grain of wheat falls to the ground and dies, it remains just a grain of wheat; but if it dies, it produces much fruit." When we've been rejected, there's only one way to go, and that's up. When we are down, we can rise. But when we are proud, we'll surely fall.

Making the most of life doesn't mean that you will be living an easy life. Rejection is hard! But if you take the rejection and turn it into an opportunity to encourage someone or to grow personally—to look someone in the eye who has rejected you and say, "Thank you. Because you rejected me, I'm a better person"—you will find that there are few things that are more fulfilling. I would love to take those who rejected me out for a thank-you dinner so that I could share with them about the many souls that have been won because of the rejection they gave me the opportunity to face. So if you are among those who have rejected me in any capacity, I owe you a free dinner and I'm excited about it!

QUOTE TO REMEMBER: "Don't you long to shout to those youths who are bustling around you: Fools! Leave those worldly things that shackle the heart—and very often degrade it—leave all that and come with us in search of Love!" —St. Josemaría Escrivá

TIME FOR GOD: Write a letter to God about a battle you are facing. Let out any frustrations you have about the challenges before you, but by the end of the letter hand over your struggles to God and let him take care of you.

MAKE IT COUNT: Ask someone you trust to pray with and for you when you are going through a tough battle. Don't worry about feeling like a burden—you will be surprised at how willing others are to help you. Your life will change when you have others in your life to help you fight your battles.

LOVE NO MATTER WHAT

Above all, hold unfailing your love for one another,
since love covers a multitude of sins.

— 1 Peter 4:8

A few years back I used to go to a barbershop here in Syracuse. The first time I entered the shop, one of the patrons asked if I was the "motherf****** po-lice." Clearly I was a little bit out of place. During a later visit, after having been given the nickname "Rev," I had a seat in Tone's chair; it was his barbershop. He pulled out the clippers and began, and while he cut, he asked me, "So, why do you really come in my barbershop?"

I said, "Man, you aren't ready to hear why I'm in your barbershop!"

He said menacingly, "Oh yeah, why don't you tell us, huh?"

I said, "I come here because it makes me uncomfortable. The way I was treated when I walked in your shop is the same way you'd be treated if you walked into the country club I grew up at."

Tone stopped dead in his tracks and said, "That's deep, bro."

From that day forward I was in. Whenever I walked in, instead of them asking if I was the po-lice, they'd say, "*Rev!* It's the reverend!" Whenever people would try to mess with me at that barbershop, Tone would say, "*Hey!* Don't mess with him—he's the Rev!"

And I would go, "Yeah! I'm the Rev!"

I can't lie; I liked it.

After going to that barbershop for a few years, one day I drove over to get a shape-up, but this would be the last time I ever went there. I sat down in Tone's chair and he looked down at me and said, "I am getting rid of the shop."

I said, "What? I love it here."

He replied, "I am not the leader I know I should be. I need to change. I need to do better."

He told me he had been selling drugs out of that barbershop. He also said he had two families and was leading a double life, and he realized he just couldn't live like that anymore. He said my message was getting to him and he had to do what was right. He ended up becoming a security guard for UPS. The last time I saw him, he told me he was so good at his job because he knew all the crooks in town!

Now, I had known that Tone was probably up to no good at times in his life. But I hadn't called him out on the wrong he was doing—all I did was encourage him throughout the years when I went to his barbershop. We are called to love others no matter what, even if they are living a lifestyle that goes against our beliefs. It is one of the most fulfilling things in the world to love someone unconditionally and to expect nothing in return, and it can have a powerful effect on others. People know when you are only caring for them in order to change them; they can sense the hidden agenda. But when we love others unconditionally for the sake of loving them and that's it, that is where we find fulfillment.

THERE'S GRACE IN THE WAIT

In my book *Win It All*, I tell the story of how my life was threatened and how I had mercy on the kid who attacked me. He was in and out of my life after that episode, but he would rarely make eye contact with me. I'd say, "Hey man, how are you?" but he'd just look the other way.

Eventually, though, I learned the power of loving no matter what when I ran into him a few years later working at a car wash. He walked right up to my window and said, "I'd like to wash your car, Justin." And I can tell you that he washed my car with such care and attention that I knew he was trying to make it up to me; he was striving to show me that we were on good terms. It was a simple gesture, but it meant a lot to me—and I think it did to him too.

I don't know what that young man is doing now, but I know the fact that I loved him no matter what even after he threatened my life made an impact on him. We have the power and the duty to show mercy to everyone in our lives, especially the ones who don't always treat us right. And although it may take years for you to have the opportunity to heal a broken relationship, that period of waiting is what sanctifies the relationship. We might get impatient or frustrated that the other person is not responding to our prayers for him or her, but there's grace in the wait. Patience deepens the love as the years go on, so when the moment for reconciliation comes, you appreciate it even more. The longer the wait, the more genuine the love. It's amazing to know that someone never gave up on you. "All this time? And yet you loved me?" That's an amazing way to love.

💡 **QUOTE TO REMEMBER:** "If the word of God is spoken by someone who is filled with the fire of charity—the fire of love of God and neighbor—it will . . . work wonders." — St. Anthony Mary Claret

✝ **TIME FOR GOD:** Spend fifteen minutes in prayer today and ask the Lord whom you need to love unconditionally. Make a list of these people in your journal so you remember to pray for them.

🎯 **MAKE IT COUNT:** Call one of those people and let them know that their life matters to you personally. Fulfillment happens when you love others with all your heart.

BE FREE

For freedom Christ set us free; stand fast therefore,
and do not submit again to a yoke of slavery.

—*Galatians 5:1*

Why should you choose to overcome the battles you face in life with Jesus as your model? Because when you are real about them and face them head-on, you find true freedom.

THE ROAD TO HEALING BEGINS WITH BEING REAL

Why should you love a father who abandoned you? One of our missionaries says, "My mind tells me to hate my dad, but my heart says that he is my father, and I'll love him forever. I'll love him even though he chose to hurt my mom, went to jail for over twenty years, and was a bad example for me." Wow! That's being real!

Many around us may be facing secret challenges. One of our missionaries has an ongoing battle with same-sex attraction. We need to stop judging those who struggle with this and start helping and encouraging them to understand how much God loves them. We have to cultivate a compassionate and understanding friendship with those bearing this heavy cross. This particular missionary knows that who he is isn't bad, but that homosexual actions are sinful. He made a decision to deal with it and not suppress it. He told his family and his close friends, and now he is free to live without giving in to temptation.

Now is the time to forgive people. Another missionary said, "My grandpa sexually abused both me and my mother, but I chose to forgive him so I can be set free." Although her mind sometimes tells her that she is junk and that she does not even deserve to be loved, her heroic decision has affected her in huge ways. Now she admits so powerfully that her grandpa is amazing, even though he hurt her, because it's not about what we do but about who we are.

Another of our missionaries went to one of the most prestigious Catholic schools in the world. On that campus a girl took advantage of her naiveté and invited her to engage in impure acts. She even quoted the Bible while she used this young woman sexually: "There is no fear in love, but perfect love drives out fear because fear has to do with punishment, and so one who fears is not yet perfect in love" (1 John 4:18). This missionary admitted her shame and received healing, and now she stands up to anyone who uses manipulative techniques to deceive. She called the girl who had hurt her and told her that what she did was wrong, but then she forgave her. Her mind said, "Hide!" But her heart said, "Deal with it!" Now she is free.

It is time to grow up and love those who have hurt you. One of our missionaries had to face his father, who had abused him. He stopped making excuses for living a mediocre life, and he stopped judging his dad. Now he and his father are loving each other in beautiful ways.

FREE OTHERS BY BEING REAL

"You will know the truth and the truth will set you free" (John 8:32). It's not easy to be real, no matter what challenges you are going through. However, it is the first way to live a life of fulfillment. Being real sometimes hurts, but it will empower you to change the world. Jesus Christ suffered on a bloody cross, and the world still wonders why. He died so that we might have life. That is why we need to go to the ends of the earth and share the reason for our hope in times of despair. We are confident that we are amazing, and yet some still may ask why.

May I be real with you? You can be confident that you are amazing, even if you've been through battles similar to those that you just read about. But it's not because of the battles or whether or not you faced them head-on. Jesus died for you so that you would know how amazing you truly are. God wouldn't have died—and didn't die—for a loser. You are amazing; that's why he died for you.

When you face your challenges and experience freedom, others will see the face of Christ in you, and therefore you will be "Jesus in disguise" for them. When you face your challenges and are set free, you will be like Christ and you will in turn set the world free by giving them the strength to face their challenges too. Now is the time—and you are the one!

💡 **QUOTE TO REMEMBER:** "If there is anyone who is not enlightened by this sublime magnificence of created things, he is blind. If there is anyone who, seeing all these works of God, does not praise Him, he is dumb; if there is anyone who, from so many signs, cannot perceive God, that man is foolish." —St. Bonaventure

✝ **TIME FOR GOD:** Admit the sin in your life, believe that God can forgive you, and commit to getting rid of that sin.

◎ **MAKE IT COUNT:** Go back to the Make It Count section of chapter one and recommit to walking through this book with a companion. If you haven't found a mentor or spiritual director yet, make it a priority to do so this week.

PART II
Be Courageous

WINNING MATTERS

*Do you not know that the runners in the stadium all run
in the race, but only one wins the prize?
Run so as to win.*

—*1 Corinthians 9:24*

Vince Lombardi is famous for saying, "Winning isn't everything. It's the only thing." It takes great courage to believe that. Jesus believed winning is everything. That is why he gave up everything to win for us. Why do we need to win? Because Jesus first won for us. The goal for winning in life is to put full trust in the mercy of God and let him guide us to victory. If we totally surrender to Jesus we are guaranteed victory. Who doesn't love a guaranteed win? Jesus already won, so let us join him.

WIN AT WHAT REALLY MATTERS

If winning didn't matter, then there would be no point in striving for heaven. Living a life of fulfillment means working our very hardest to win the prize of eternal life with God our Father. By winning at how God has called us to live here on earth, we will win the ultimate prize.

In *Win It All*, the book I wrote in 2010, I reflect on eight ways to get to heaven. If winning heaven matters to you, then you can start with these:

1. Recognize your importance.
2. Discover God's plan for your life.
3. Make your negative mess a positive message.
4. Be passionate.
5. Remain fearless.
6. Commit to loving others.
7. Never give up.
8. Live every day as if it were your last.

These eight points give us a simple way to live a life of fulfillment. Look over them with a sincere heart and reflect on how you can incorporate them into your life.

DON'T WIN FOR YOURSELF

The greatest way to encourage someone is to win for him or her. When I speak to college football teams, I ask them this question: "Who are you going to win for?" The athletes will say things like, "I want to win for my mother who's dying of cancer, my brother who got shot, my friend who didn't get the opportunity I did to go to college." Winning for someone matters. When we win for others, it empowers us on a whole new level. Winning is hard because often we want to give up when it seems like we are going to lose. It is even harder when it seems like we are down in life 44-0. All the odds are against us, but if we read the Old Testament, time and time again the odds were against these characters too. Jonah found himself in the belly of the whale, but with God he was able to pull out the victory (see Jonah 1–3). Ruth did the impossible with God's help. She was not a victim—she was a victor (see the book of Ruth). When Abraham trusted God, he won: God spared his son Isaac and made Abraham the father of the faith—with more descendants than any man who ever lived (see Genesis 22).

Whom will you win for?

QUOTE TO REMEMBER: "Holiness is not for wimps and the cross is not negotiable, sweetheart, it's a requirement." —Mother Angelica

TIME FOR GOD: Spend fifteen minutes in prayer today and ask God to help you win in key areas of your life where you are struggling. Ask a mentor or trusted companion to keep you accountable in these areas.

MAKE IT COUNT: Write down in your journal five ways to improve your community by being generous with your time and money. Help out at a soup kitchen, babysit for a couple who could use a date night, volunteer at a nursing home, make a donation to a charity. When you give back to your community you realize that life is not all about you.

ANYTHING IS POSSIBLE

Little children, you are of God, and have overcome them;
for he who is in you is greater than he who is in the world.

—*1 John 4:4*

THE COURAGE OF GIDEON

Gideon was a lot like many of us—he doubted his own abilities to do what God asked of him. He had experienced defeat and failure, but God had a lesson to teach him.

But the Lord told Gideon, "There are still too many! Bring them down to the spring, and I will test them to determine who will go with you and who will not." When Gideon took his warriors down to the water, the Lord told him, "Divide the men into two groups. In one group put all those who cup water in their hands and lap it up with their tongues like dogs. In the other group put all those who kneel down and drink with their mouths in the stream." Only 300 of the men drank from their hands. All the others got down on their knees and drank with their mouths in the stream. (Judges 7:4–6)

The Israelites had offended God by worshipping other gods. Needless to say, drastic measures needed to be taken. Just before this passage, in Judges 6:12, the Lord called Gideon through an angel: "The Lord is with you, O mighty man of valor!" For the previous seven years, the Israelites had been destroyed by the Midianites, in whose land they were delivered, so naturally Gideon wondered, "How am I going to deliver my people out of this when God has not been with us?" But God himself told Gideon, "Go in this might of yours and deliver Israel from the hand of Midian; do not I send you?" (verse 14).

Gideon pleaded with God, asking, "Who, me?" Just like Moses, Peter, and you and me, Gideon stopped in his tracks and thought, *How am I going to do this?* Only with a vast amount of courage and determination could he trust in God to pull off this mission. Right off the bat, the people wanted to kill him because he had destroyed an altar to a false god. When the battle ensued, Gideon was up against thirty thousand warriors, with many fewer of his own. And, as if those odds were not enough to glorify God with an underdog win, God pushed Gideon to trust his power even further. God did it. He won the fight for Gideon's army.

YOUR FIGHT

When you have the courage to trust in God like Gideon did, you can conquer anything. Gideon took the promise of the Lord's power and challenged the Israelite people, calling them out of their sin and shame. God is looking for those who, like Gideon, truly follow and listen to his voice no matter what he is asking of them. When we follow God's commands, we can conquer whatever battle is before us, no matter how massive the army is. Gideon stuck with what God was asking him to do even though the battle seemed impossible, and that allowed God to win the battle. It was all because of Gideon's strong grip on the power that was unleashed when he trusted in the Lord.

Maybe you are looking at a particular task at hand and asking, "How in the world can this be accomplished?" We need to put our trust in the Lord and follow his plan for us. "Not my will, but thine, be done" (Luke 22:42). Then the Holy Spirit will place a never-say-die courage in us, and we can conquer anything—sin, death, addiction, or any other struggle that is in our path to eternal joy. Through the power of the Lord Almighty, anything is possible!

"INCONVENIENT" MOMENTS

I was waiting in line at Starbucks in North Jersey, and as I observed the employees, I could tell they needed encouragement. The place was packed with people waiting to get their high-octane drinks, and all I wanted was a Rice Krispies Treat. I don't know about you, but I love Rice Krispies Treats; my life is just so much better when I have them. (Maybe I'll add Rice Krispies Treats as the sixth way to make the most of life . . .) I've even had people send me homemade Rice Krispies Treats after an event to thank me—and they are my favorite people!

I finally got to the front of the line and said, "Could I have a Rice Krispies Treat?" And she said the worst thing that you can say to a Rice Krispies Treat lover: "I'm sorry, sir, we are all out." I looked up at her with a deflated expression on my face and said, "My life sucks."

She looked at me and responded, "My life sucks too, sir."

Instantly, in my heart of hearts, I said to God, "We've got a *live* one here!" My heart of courage kicked in. I looked back at the line of Scrooge-like Starbucks fanatics and thought to myself, overcame my fear, and said to the employee, "Could I pray with you?" She said, "Sure, sir!" I bowed my head (trying not to worry about the disgruntled un-caffeinated creatures behind me), and I prayed with all my heart that she would know how much God loves her.

The other employee behind the counter said, "My name's Terry. Could you pray for me too?"

I agreed, and what do you know? We had a healing service right there in the Starbucks line! Anything is possible. Changing the world through encouragement happens one person at a time. It's not through a program at your church, not through a conference you attend—it's through your daily interactions with those around you. It's loving that one person in front of you like Christ, every time.

QUOTE TO REMEMBER: "Start by doing what's necessary; then do what's possible; and suddenly you are doing the impossible." —St. Francis of Assisi

✝ **TIME FOR GOD:** Pray the St. Michael Prayer today:

> *St. Michael the Archangel, defend us in battle.*
> *Be our defense against the wickedness and snares of the Devil.*
> *May God rebuke him, we humbly pray, and do thou,*
> *O Prince of the heavenly hosts, by the power of God,*
> *thrust into hell Satan, and all the evil spirits,*
> *who prowl about the world seeking the ruin of souls.*
> *Amen.*

🎯 **MAKE IT COUNT:** Have the courage to ask someone if you can pray out loud for him or her, even when you think it might not be the right time to do so. God always honors an act of courage.

FACING SIN TAKES GUTS

"For the wages of sin is death, but the free gift of God is eternal life in Christ Jesus our Lord."

—Romans 6:23

Many people have a hard time admitting their sinfulness. If this is the case for you, you can use what I call the ABCs of Christianity to help you.

Admit it: Admitting our sin to ourselves, God, and others is the first step in unlocking the beautiful power of repentance in our lives. Being repentant means that we change direction, turn away from the unhealthy habits and actions in our lives, and come back to God. True repentance doesn't mean "I will *try* to change"—it means "I *will* change." We change by going to confession and being honest about every sin we have committed, and then believing that Christ can forgive us for anything and everything.

Believe it: If we don't have faith that God will forgive us, he won't force it on us. Forgiveness is a free gift, but we have to accept it in order to receive it. True transformation happens when we stop making excuses and have the guts to make a plan to change our lives and stick to it.

Commit to it: If you know that going to a party will tempt you to get drunk, commit to staying away from the party scene. If you know that keeping your phone by your bed is going to cause you to look at things that are sinful, commit to keeping your phone somewhere else at night. In order to face our sinfulness, we must decide to make practical, positive changes in our daily lives.

THE BEST PLACE TO START

What if the only thing that mattered was being real, knowing that God is real, and being absolutely confident that he loves you? That's it! What if you could look people in the eyes and tell them it doesn't matter whether they judge you or not? What matters is the fact that you love them because you were first loved by God. The best place to start is in confession. Some of us hear that word and automatically think, *No way!* But this sacrament allows us to be 100 percent authentic and, as I like to say, "let it rip!" Confession is the place where you're going to begin to get your kid heart back.

When you make a mistake and go to confession, it's all over. It's just like telling your parents when you made a mistake when you were a kid, but instead you're telling God the Father (the best dad ever). If you come to God and truly desire to change, he will always forgive you. In confession we receive the grace of his divine mercy. Confession gives you an opportunity to look at your life and ask yourself if you are ready to be the best, most real version of yourself. You'll start to realize that so many things you think matter really don't, while the things you tend to forget about matter the most. Leave the past behind; focus on the new, and experience a whole new level of hope and fulfillment.

💡 **QUOTE TO REMEMBER:** "Saints are sinners who kept on going." —Robert Louis Stevenson

✝ **TIME FOR GOD:** Be courageous and go to confession today (even if it's been years since you've gone), and let it all out. Confession has never killed anyone. Sin kills and confession gives fulfillment. I never met anyone who died from going to confession.

🎯 **MAKE IT COUNT:** Don't go to confession just once—develop the habit of going at least once a month. Every two weeks is even better. You might take a risk and invite someone to go with you.

SUCCESSFUL CONFRONTATION

*Set your heart right and be steadfast, incline your ear, and
receive words of understanding, and do not be hasty
in time of calamity.*

—Sirach 2:2

It's one thing to face what's wrong in our own lives, but it requires courage to confront other people when issues crop up in our friendships, businesses, churches, and families. This is never easy, and many of us shy away from this type of honesty in our relationships.

However, confrontation isn't always about big, hairy issues. Sometimes it's about facing the little details of life that cause disharmony and discord, and then working through those collaboratively. Confrontation keeps us from carrying anger, which is a lot like drinking poison and expecting the other person to get sick.

Following is a basic strategy for being courageous and successful in our confrontations with others.

A MODEL FOR SUCCESSFUL CONFRONTATION

1. Before confronting someone, focus first and foremost on loving that person. Ask God how to love this individual as Christ would.

2. Once you are ready to love like Christ, meet with this person ASAP to discuss the issue. Don't wait!

3. If the person is open to it, start by saying a prayer together to begin your meeting. It is always good to bring God into the center of conflicts. If the other person isn't open to that, say a prayer on your own, asking God to bless the conversation and make it fruitful.

4. Listen intently to what the other person has to say about the situation and really try to understand. Don't just wait for him or her to finish so you can speak.

5. After listening, repeat to the person what you heard to let him or her know you understand what was shared. Then explain the issues as you see them, and discuss. Be clear and concise, and stay focused on the topic at hand; do not make it personal!

6. Next, agree on an action plan with concrete steps to resolve the situation. This is the time to set any necessary boundaries within your relationship.

7. After you are in agreement with the action plan and the boundaries established, set up a time to meet again to see if the situation has been resolved. If it hasn't, go back to step one to work on any unresolved issues.

Note: It might also be helpful to ask one other person to sit in on your meeting. That way, once the meeting is over and the tension has settled, that person can keep you both accountable regarding the boundaries you set and remind you to keep the agreements you made.

QUOTE TO REMEMBER: "Conflict is inevitable, but combat is optional." —Max Lucado

TIME FOR GOD: Ask God if there is anyone you need to confront. If so, ask him for the right words to say and the courage to speak up for what is right. Journal about your feelings regarding this confrontation.

MAKE IT COUNT: When and if you identify the need to confront that person, follow the Model for Successful Confrontation so that you can find peace and fulfillment in your relationship.

Observe the people in your life and be willing to be a third-party monitor in order to help others succeed in confrontation. It is such a fulfilling experience knowing that you've helped someone get through a tough confrontation.

SUFFER WELL

*No temptation has overtaken you that is not common
to man. God is faithful, and he will not let you be tempted
beyond your strength, but with the temptation will also
provide the way of escape, that you may be able to endure it.*

—*1 Corinthians 10:13*

THE CORONADO BRIDGE

For years I traveled to San Diego, California, to meet with the Johnsons, a family with five kids: four girls and a boy, named Michael. The Johnson family brought so much hope and encouragement to my life and to the lives of many others. Each year, they would house, feed, and spend time with my missionary team and me . We would hang out and have a great time—they even sent us to Sea World once because they had a connection to get us in for free. Every time I left their house, I felt so cared for.

One day one of my office assistants handed me the stack of mail that had come in that day. Many situations in life teach us to suffer well, and I was about to encounter one of them. I opened a letter from Mr. Johnson. It read, "I wish I could have told you at the time when this happened, but with everything going on . . . well, I apologize for waiting to tell you this. My son, Michael, ended his life—he jumped off the Coronado Bridge. I am devastated. My wife and I have been through so much suffering losing our precious son. My daughters, my wife, and I are just wondering, 'Why? How did this happen?'"

The letter continued, "Justin, you were one of the first people I thought about when Michael took his life. All that you have been saying about the pain and suffering people go through— well, I've found out just how real it is." Mr. Johnson also shared with me that two of his daughters, who had both entered religious life, decided to leave the convent so they could receive the healing they needed along with their family. He asked me to pray that his family could find God's will in all of this as they struggled to move forward.

I was so devastated when I read this letter from Mr. Johnson; it brought back my own recent despair when my friend Andy had tried to kill himself—except my friend had survived. The Johnson family's story was heartbreaking.

THE COURAGEOUS AFTERMATH

What Michael did by ending his life on the Coronado Bridge was not what God intended. However, God, in all his goodness, can take even a horrific situation like this and bring hope from it. After I had read the letter from Mr. Johnson that day, I looked back and realized that Andy—who had been released from the hospital just a few days before—knew the Johnson family. He had been working with Michael over the phone after meeting him on a trip we were on together.

I had Andy read the letter, and I believe that it has given him the strength to never give up on his own life again. Andy told me he realized that there are so many people hurting in this world, and they need the hope that only Jesus Christ has to offer.

In this case, just as in many others, God used a horrible situation to inspire courage in someone else. Suffering well means taking a bad situation for what it is and bringing good from it, rather than letting the negative parts win out. When we suffer well, God gets the glory. Andy can suffer well now, knowing that what Michael chose was not the answer because of the devastation it caused his family. Andy is not going to give up on himself again, no matter how much he may suffer, because he knows his life on this earth matters. That is suffering for a purpose, and that is suffering well.

Mr. and Mrs. Johnson decided to share their story with others to help those who have family or friends who have attempted or committed suicide. They even came to our missionary training and shared their story about how God can use all our sufferings to encourage others, in hopes that their son's death would never be in vain. One missionary looked the mother in the eye and said, "I wanted to jump off a bridge too. But meeting you now, I'm so glad I didn't."

A deacon from the Johnsons' church told them his son had also taken his own life. You see, Michael's end on earth was still used to bring healing to others because that deacon now knows he is not alone. The only way such heavy trials can bring hope is the mystery of the cross, and it takes a brave heart to embrace the cross and learn how to suffer well. With the "you're amazing" message we always go back to the scripture verse Ezekiel 36:26 when someone is going through suffering: "I will give you a new heart, and a new spirit I will put within you. I will remove the heart of stone from your flesh and give you a heart of flesh." The meaning of the Greek translation for *flesh* is "carnal," or "tender heart." To have a fulfilled heart we need to keep it tender daily, regardless of how much it might hurt. It is almost always through suffering that God is able to get us to a point where we are ready to receive this new tender heart. We all go through pain and suffering, but we also all have the choice to suffer poorly or suffer well. When we make the choice to suffer well, God softens our hearts so that we can receive the great gifts he has in store for us.

But why suffer well? If suffering is pointless, useless, and just a downright hassle with no meaning, then by all means, suffer poorly! But what if there is a deeper meaning in every pain and trial you endure? Suffering in and of itself has no meaning, but it can always direct us to something that has value. For example, pain is often an indicator that something is wrong or needs attention. When your throat hurts, it could mean that you are getting sick. If you have a headache, it could mean many different things. When God allows suffering in your life, it is always going to point you to something greater than the pain you feel. We know this is true because God chose to suffer on Calvary as a means of pointing us to salvation and holiness. In fact, he shows us that suffering is the preferred path to holiness. Every cross can be turned into a resurrection if we choose to suffer well, and the only way to suffer well is to suffer with Christ. He teaches us that we are not meant to suffer alone; even he suffered with his mother and St. John at the foot of the cross. When we suffer we need to ask God for the grace to admit it, accept it, and endure it. This is how we are going to begin to see the blessing in the midst of any pain we go through. When we suffer well we will live well, but if we live well that does not necessarily mean we will suffer well.

💡 **QUOTE TO REMEMBER:** "If you really want to love Jesus, first learn to suffer, because suffering teaches you to love." —St. Gemma

✝ **TIME FOR GOD:** Ask God for the grace to admit, accept, and endure the greatest challenge facing you today. Make a commitment to face each suffering with courage from now on.

◎ **MAKE IT COUNT:** Think of someone who has suffered well, and share with him or her how it has brought you hope in your own journey. The "You're Amazing" message brings encouragement especially to those who are suffering well.

NEVER GIVE UP

Moses said to the people, "Fear not, stand firm, and see the
salvation of the Lord, which he will work for you today; for
the Egyptians whom you see today,
you shall never see again."

—*Exodus 14:13*

MY WIFE, MARY

I was sitting with my grandmother one day. I had a pizzelle in
one hand and a diet coke in the other. As she drank her daily cup
of coffee, she said to me, "Justin, how did you know not to give up
on pursuing that girl you married?"

I said, "Grandma, it was God's grace!"

The day I graduated from Cathedral Preparatory School, an all-
boys school in Erie, Pennsylvania, I took my diploma and handed
it to my mother—because, let's be real here, there is no way I would
have made it through without her help! When I handed it to her,

she said, "Justin, you can keep the diploma, but when you go to college, meet a smart girl and spend a lot of time with her because she'll be the one who will get you through college."

That fall, as a college freshman at Seton Hall University, in South Orange, New Jersey, I took my mother's advice and found that smart girl to get me through college. I knew she was the one because she was wearing glasses—and she even had freckles! But little did I know that I would soon fall in love with my new "tutor." It had been two years since I'd kissed a girl, because when I decided to follow Christ with my whole heart, I chose to be pure. My spiritual mentor, Father Larry Richards, told me that nobody was going to marry me anyway because no one would be able to deal with me! But after spending so much time with the beautiful and smart Mary Zimmerman, I kissed her and we began moving forward in our relationship.

Fast-forward a few years, and Mary and I were ready to graduate college. My grades were excellent, we had a great relationship, and college had been a blast. But I started to get nervous about what the future would hold if I continued in my relationship with Mary: marriage. Gulp! Was I ready for that? I was so confused and didn't know what I was called to do with my life, so I decided to break up with her halfway through our last semester.

When I broke up with Mary, I was so nervous that I ended up saying some pretty dumb things. She started crying, and I blurted out, "Why are you crying? I need to test-drive other cars!" That was a mistake; her hurt instantly turned into anger—which made me even more uncomfortable, so I said, "Why are you so upset?

I have to shop the market!" This did not help. (Quick tip: Men, learn from me—do not use either of those lines, ever!)

But two weeks later, after realizing that there was no woman who could even come close to comparing with Mary, I resolved to win her heart back. When I saw her on campus, I told her, "You're the one, Mary! I'm sorry for breaking up with you. I know I'm supposed to marry you! We have to get back together."

She looked at me and said, "Don't talk to me and don't e-mail me—I don't want to see you."

I said, "For how long?"

"I don't know."

I was crushed. But as successful confrontation has taught us, when you make an agreement, you need to stick to the boundaries that are set. I went through the next two months seeing her but not being able to communicate with her, and it was really hard. I finally called Fr. Larry, crying—and he started to laugh!

"What are you laughing at?"

"Son, you will never be able to preach the Gospel unless you have a broken heart."

He was right.

I resolved to respect the boundaries she had set. When she went to the senior prom with my former roommate, rather than asking another girl to be my date, I took a homeless man out to dinner. This made me feel a little better, but still, I missed Mary. Almost three months later, she walked up to me and invited me to sit with her at graduation. I thought, I've got a shot!

After graduation, she said, "Justin, if you think you have so much to offer me, why don't you put it on paper?" She told me to call her in a month to talk. During that time, I worked on my essay: "What I Have to Offer My Future Wife." I sent it to Mary one month later. I also had kept a journal during the four-month period when we were apart, and I titled it "The Days without Mary."

And now we are married and have five children—the rest is history in the making. She was worth the fight; she was worth not giving up on. But it took a lot of perseverance. If I had given up the first time she rejected me, I wouldn't be enjoying the great life I have with her and our kids now. God is good, and he always honors perseverance—so never give up!

QUOTE TO REMEMBER: "I plead with you—never, ever give up on hope, never doubt, never tire, and never become discouraged. Be not afraid." —St. John Paul II

TIME FOR GOD: Pray for a mentor or companion who has been willing to work to make a difference in your life and the lives of others. Then ask this person if he or she would be willing to pray for you daily. It takes courage to ask others to pray for you and you to pray for others. We can't reach a life of fulfillment alone.

MAKE IT COUNT: Is there a relationship in your life that you're tempted to give up on? How about a situation that you're afraid to tackle because of a fear of failure? Ask God for strength—and then go for it!

OFFER IT UP

I appeal to you therefore, brethren, by the mercies of God, to present your bodies as a living sacrifice, holy and acceptable to God, which is your spiritual worship. Do not be conformed to this world but be transformed by the renewal of your mind, that you may prove what is the will of God, what is good and acceptable and perfect.

—Romans 12:1–2

If you were looking for some light reading, you might be thinking that this book is getting a little too heavy for you. But my goal is to show you how you can take the heaviness of life that you already have and make it a little lighter. If we ignore the suffering around us, it might seem lighter at first, but nine times out of ten, it will come back to hit us even harder. Sometimes it has to get harder before it gets easier, so bear with me.

"Wait, what? Now you want me to suffer *more*? This seems counterintuitive!" Yes. The cross is a paradox. Although it is a cross, it is also the means to our salvation. If we suffer with a reason, our load becomes lighter—and what better reason than to save souls? Who in your life needs a miracle? Offer up your suffering for them, and watch what God does with it. Miracles will start happening—just wait!

St. Thérèse would often "offer up" all of the small inconveniences and annoyances of her day for suffering souls. Her mother taught her to keep sacrifice beads, and every time she sacrificed something for another person and offered it up as a prayer, she would slide one bead over to keep count throughout the day. St. Paul said we are privileged to share in the sufferings of Christ: "Now I rejoice in my sufferings for your sake, and in my flesh I complete what is lacking in Christ's afflictions for the sake of his body, that is, the church" (Colossians 1:24).

This is a way for us, as Catholics, to pray for others. So often, we live our lives totally unaware of the suffering that is all around us—and we waste the opportunity to share our grace! What if, instead of getting ticked off at the driver in front of us who is going too slow, we prayed for him and his family because they might be going through a tough time? What if every time we had to wait in line and started to get impatient, we prayed for the cashier who is stuck there all day, who is perhaps working that job to provide for her kids? What if every time we stubbed our toe or got sick, we prayed for someone who has cancer? What if whenever we had a conflict with someone, we ate something we don't particularly like and offered it up for their suffering?

Every day in our office we want to share the "You're Amazing" message, so we bless ourselves and slap a sign with the words of the daily prayer we pray to offer up our work for suffering souls: "Lord Jesus, I give you my life, through pain, through suffering, and through joy." It's time to get creative about offering up inconveniences and trials so we can save more souls and grow the heavenly kingdom of God. The external sacrifices and mortifications, whether necessary or voluntary, are what ultimately convert our hearts and cause us to have interior conversions; offering it up will help us get there too.

THE POWER OF THE PRAYER WORKOUT

Twice a week, every week, my team and I wake up before the rest of the world to offer up a workout for the people in our lives who are suffering. The missionaries and office team are there every time, but we also open up the workout to the larger Syracuse community.

One of our mission supporters in the area, who recently experienced the unfailing love of Christ in her life, often joins us and she sometimes brings her friends so they can experience this powerful love for themselves. During a Tuesday morning prayer workout, one of her friends, Abby, was greatly impacted. Abby was quiet but focused for most of the workout. She loved to exercise, but she had never experienced a workout in which the focus was not all on you, but on other people. Toward the end of the workout, when we were already exhausted, I challenged the team to run sprints for someone they needed to forgive. Unexpectedly Abby spoke up and said, "My ex." She had been holding on to the pain of breaking up with her boyfriend of a year and a half. It had been three months since they had broken up, and she was struggling with letting it go. Abby gave it all she had, and by the time the team closed in prayer, she had tears rolling down her face. As she walked away with a new feeling in her heart, she shared that she had never felt anything like that before. Afterward the friend who had brought her told us that she had known Abby since they were children, and she had never seen her cry. Offering up sacrifices for others can change our hearts too.

QUOTE TO REMEMBER: "You will be consoled according to the greatness of your sorrow and affliction; the greater the suffering, the greater will be the reward." —St. Mary Magdalene de Pazzi

TIME FOR GOD: Pray the Morning Prayer with St. Thérèse of Lisieux:

O my God! I offer Thee all my actions of this day for the intentions and for the glory of the Sacred Heart of Jesus. I desire to sanctify every beat of my heart, my every thought, my simplest works, by uniting them to His infinite merits; and I wish to make reparation for my sins by casting them into the furnace of His merciful love. O my God, I ask of Thee for myself and for those dear to me the grace to fulfill perfectly Thy holy will, to accept, for love of Thee, the joys and sorrows of

*this passing life, so that we may one day be united together in
Heaven for all eternity.
Amen.*

MAKE IT COUNT: Work out (take a walk, go for a run, go to
the gym) as a prayer for someone who is suffering. When
we put the focus on others and not ourselves, we find
fulfillment.

LISTEN TO OUR ADVERSARIES

"Everyone then who hears these words of mine and does them will be like a wise man who built his house on the rock."

—*Matthew 7:24*

SHUT UP TIME

It is easy to pray and talk to God about what is on our hearts, but to be still and listen takes courage—because sometimes we might not like what we hear, even though it's what is best for us. The ability to set aside time and space to listen in this loud world is limited. Fr. Larry Richards bluntly calls listening to God his "shut up time." We all need to shut up and unplug everything around us in order to hear God. Listening to God is not just meditation, or some routine thought process; it's being in communion and in a relationship with a God who dwells within us. God's answers come in many forms: a verbal or written word, a person who shows up in our lives, a moment of realization, a phone call exactly when we need it, Divine Providence, the gift of nature around us, and so much more. But it is his whispers that draw us ever closer to heaven.

This kind of listening takes courage. I always ask atheists and agnostics if they've ever just sat in silence and tried listening to God. Many of them have not. I guarantee that those who take the time to listen end up having faith if they are persistent enough. Listening to God during shut up time is the essential piece that separates a believer from a nonbeliever. When you've spent silent time with God, you will be full of joy because you have a personal relationship with a loving God, a God who listens to us: our questions, our concerns, and what is in the depths of our hearts. He knows us through and through.

GOD MOVES POWERFULLY IN THE SILENCE

During a conference I attended, one of the leaders bashed me and my organization in front of hundreds of people. If I had given in to my own thoughts in that moment, I would have bashed him back—and probably poked him in the eyes! But I decided to shut up instead and listen to God. I realized that the only reason he could say something so hurtful was that he had gone through something hurtful himself.

I decided to sit next to this guy at lunch and ask him how I could do better. During the conversation, we realized that we both played tennis. I asked him if we could play sometime. He said that he lived roughly seven hundred miles from me and didn't think it would be possible. I said, "We have a bus. I'll stop by and we can play when I'm in your area."

The next time we were in his area, the missionaries and I met him at a Chick-fil-A (in my opinion, one of the more amazing fast-food restaurants). We ended up talking about the greatest challenges we faced in our lives. He shared about how his daughter had been abused recently. I remembered how he had bashed me in front of all those people, and I realized that he struggled with me because he cared about his daughter and wanted to be sure I was genuinely loving people and caring for them. That day he shared with me a great communication model, which we have been using in our trainings ever since. God is so funny—sometimes he uses the strangest characters to help fulfill his plan for our lives.

QUOTE TO REMEMBER: "When it's God who is speaking . . . the proper way to behave is to imitate someone who has an irresistible curiosity and who listens at keyholes. You must listen to everything God says at the keyhole of your heart." —St. John Vianney

TIME FOR GOD: Pray for your adversaries (enemies) daily. Make a list in your journal of people you struggle with and those who struggle with you. Ask God for ways to love them in amazing ways.

MAKE IT COUNT: Winston Churchill said, "Courage is what it takes to stand up and speak; courage is also what it takes to sit down and listen." Practice listening to someone important in your life for fifteen minutes every day. Do this for fifteen days and watch how your relationship with him or her blossoms! A life of fulfillment is all about having the courage to listen to those we love. Practice listening to those you love, and then summon the courage to listen to your adversaries. Find a way to make an enemy your friend.

PART III
Be Prayerful

YOUR INTERIOR LIFE

*Mary . . . sat at the Lord's feet and listened to his
teaching. . . . "There is need of only one thing. Mary has
chosen the good portion, which shall not be
taken away from her."*

—Luke 10:39, 42

What does it take for you to feel content? Many of us think that
in order to be content in life, we need to make sure that every
desire of ours is filled. We think that if we accomplish this
or that, then we will be truly happy. But what I discovered is
that a relationship with Jesus Christ is the only thing that *truly*
satisfies; I learned that he is the source of true contentment.
If you put **J**esus first, **O**thers second, and **Y**ourself last, that's
how you get **JOY!**

But practically speaking, how do you really put Jesus
first? The only way I know is by spending time with him.

The way we do that is through daily prayer; we work on our relationship with God through our internal conversations with him, through cultivating our interior life.

Deep inside we can enjoy a supernatural experience on a daily basis during our time in prayer and as we go through the day with Jesus. Cultivating our interior life increases faith, hope, and love within us, enabling us to impact everyone in our world in a positive, life-changing way. It empowers us to resist temptation and handle the difficulties we face each day with confidence and joy. When we have a strong interior life, we see life through God's eyes, and it is certainly worth the discipline it takes to develop this.

Dom Sebastian Wyart, a French abbot who died in 1904, said there are three kinds of labor:

1. Manual labor: physical labor; this is the easiest of all three.
2. Mental labor: intellectual toil, thinking work; this is more difficult than manual labor.
3. Interior labor: cultivating the life of the soul; this not only is the most demanding, it is the most important kind of labor and offers us the most satisfaction here on earth.

Even though physical labor can be intense, and thinking labor is very demanding, the labor of the interior life is by far the most difficult. Why? Because you have to dominate your mind, your inner self (your heart), *and* your environment in order to achieve inner mastery. You have to direct all your energy to maintain your union with Jesus and stay focused. As Wyart said, paraphrasing St. Ignatius, "And so everything in [you], intelligence and will as well as memory, feelings, imagination, and senses depends on principle. But to achieve an interior life, what an effort it would cost [you]!"

Think about it: What takes more energy? Waiting patiently still for God's voice during your silent prayer time and fighting the battles in your own head and heart, or being a preacher speaking to thousands of people, saying the right things and getting a standing ovation? As hard as it is to preach, it takes a lot more focus, a lot more concentration, and a lot more determination to persevere in prayer.

But is it worth the effort? I'd say so! Every saint had a strong and consistent interior life—no matter their personality, spirituality, or accomplishments (or lack thereof) while on earth. They were saints *because* of their interior lives of prayer and union with God. Even if they accomplished a great deal, it was because they kept themselves in union with God and let him work through them. Our true power is the power of Christ in us, and we can tap into that by developing a strong inner life.

The interior life is what overcomes our inclination to sin. It is our greatest source of strength. It is a reservoir, gushing forth the power of Christ into our very being and out to those around us. It will give us joy even in the midst of the trials, temptations, and challenges. We will not lose our joy even when we are in the thick of the busyness of life, in the thick of disease, or in the thick of any hardship we face.

FIVE FACTS ABOUT THE INTERIOR LIFE

1. When you have a consistent interior life, you realize that what other people ask of you is insignificant compared to what Jesus asks of you.
2. Your interior life can be compared to a plant's stem, filled with rich nutrients that produce beautiful flowers—the fruit you bear in your life for Jesus.
3. Every time you go within, you increase the power of Christ within you, and that has a significant impact on the choices you make.
4. Your prayer life is more beneficial than any work you do.
5. What is the relationship between the interior life and the active life? A person with an interior life is a contemplative in action.

The way we are going to win our own soul is through our interior life. If we don't cultivate a strong inner life with Christ, there will be no way we can help others to do so. Like anything that takes discipline, the more you procrastinate, the harder it is to get started. You might think, *There's too much to be done! I don't have time for prayer!* But just like the saints who have gone before us, we know that prayer is the last thing we ought to neglect when we are busy. St. Francis de Sales said, "Every one of us needs a half an hour of prayer each day, except when we are busy—then we need an hour."

💡 **QUOTE TO REMEMBER:** "Satan . . . on the contrary, does not hesitate to encourage a purely superficial success, if he can by this success prevent the apostle from making progress in the interior life." —Jean-Baptiste Chautard, OCSO, *The Soul of the Apostolate*

✝ **TIME FOR GOD:** Sit in silence for five minutes every day for a week when you wake up. Set your timer for five minutes and just listen to God. Write down what you sense the Lord saying to you. This will help you develop your interior life. When you succeed in that, up the time to ten, fifteen, or even twenty minutes. Make it your long-term goal to do a holy hour once a day for ninety days straight.

🎯 **MAKE IT COUNT:** Who is on your heart today? Tell that person how he or she came to your mind while you were having your daily silent time. Be honest about how you are searching for a more fulfilling life.

HOUR OF POWER

*And he came to the disciples and found them sleeping;
and he said to Peter, "So, could you not watch
with me one hour?"*

—Matthew 26:40

START SMALL

Prayer can be intimidating if at first you bite off more than you can chew. But think of prayer like beginning to work out after taking a long hiatus from physical activity: You have to ease into it. We have all resolved to exercise more often, and we know that the beginning is difficult, but the more we work out, the more we desire to and the more we even enjoy it. You will be more successful this way. Archbishop Fulton J. Sheen said, "It is not particularly difficult to find thousands who will spend two or three hours a day in exercising, but if you ask them to bend their knees to God in five minutes of prayer, they protest that it is too long." Well, the good news is that five minutes is all you need to start with in order to be successful in prayer!

One of our team members explained that if you want to get into the habit of working out, get up early every day, put on your workout clothes and sneakers, and sit on the couch for an hour—for twenty-one days straight. You might be thinking, *Wow, I can do that!* Well, you're right. Because after about a week, you're going to feel silly just sitting on the couch when you are already dressed and ready to work out. Soon you'll be running for five minutes, then ten, and then maybe even lifting weights too. Before you know it, you'll be in shape.

Prayer works the same way. If you begin with an hour when you've never prayed before or after taking substantial time off from prayer, you will get discouraged and think, *I can't do this.* Instead, start by getting up early to pray during the "heroic minute," the first minute you are awake in the morning. Once you've gotten into the habit of praying for that first minute, bump it up to five minutes. Soon you'll be well on your way to cultivating a deep interior life of prayer.

THE FIVE-MINUTE PRAYER

Spend one minute praying about each topic:

    a. Tell God what you're sorry for.
    b. Tell God what you're thankful for.
    c. Tell God your prayer requests.
    d. Surrender to God.
    e. Listen to God in silence.

BE A HERO

The heroic minute is called "heroic" because for some people it is a serious battle. St. John Vianney said, "We must take great care never to do anything before having said our morning prayers. . . . The devil once declared that if he could have the first moment of the day, he was sure to have all the rest." For people struggling with depression, getting out of bed can be the biggest challenge they face during the day. If you can conquer that first minute, the other fifty-nine will be much easier, and soon, with God's grace, you will conquer the rest of your day.

Even Jesus took time away from the distractions of life to focus on his relationship with God. He would get up early or move away from the crowds in order to be with his Father, listen to him, and be filled by his Spirit. Each day our goal should be to give the Lord an hour of prayer. Sometimes it is a challenge to figure out when and where and how to get that hour in. You might have to break it up—you could pray for five minutes when you wake up, twenty-five minutes while you drive to work, twenty minutes while you're folding socks, and ten minutes before you go to bed.

If you are blessed with a full hour that is open during the day, there are many ways you can approach prayer. In fact, there isn't a wrong way to pray if you are truly seeking to do the will of God. During a prayer hour you can start with entering into God's presence by praising him and thanking him. You can read the Scriptures—maybe something from Psalms or Proverbs or the New Testament. You might want to write out one of the verses on an index card or type it into your phone so you have it with you all day. At the end of the day, take a few minutes to evaluate how you're living your life, and confess any sins (see 1 John 1:9). Make a list of people you want to pray for and keep it on your phone or in your journal.

Practice sitting in silence. And then, when your mind and heart have settled, ask God a question or two each day. For example, you might ask him, "How can I love my wife better?" Then really listen—not with your ears, but with your heart—for his answer. When you get distracted, listen again. Recognize the distraction that pops up as a distraction and leave it at that. You don't need to ignore it or keep pushing it away; just let it float away while you get back to prayer. Record what God tells you for that day in a journal so you can go back to the truths he has spoken to you during your prayer time. Pray for your family, your leaders, your enemies, and your coworkers. Close by giving thanks to God—always end with gratitude.

Whatever methods you use, just don't leave out the two most important aspects of prayer: silence and the Word of God. These are the pillars that your interior life will be grounded in.

QUOTE TO REMEMBER: "God, give us grace to accept with serenity the things that cannot be changed, courage to change the things that should be changed, and the wisdom to distinguish the one from the other." —Reinhold Niebuhr

TIME FOR GOD: Practice the five-minute prayer and see if you can increase your time to at least ten minutes today. Stay committed!

MAKE IT COUNT: Three answers to prayer:
1. Yes!
2. Not yet.
3. No, I have something better in mind.

Write down the toughest questions you have for God. Look back after you are done reading this book and see if God has answered any of your questions with a yes, a no, or an "I have something better in mind."

FESTIVAL OF SILENCE

Even a fool who keeps silent is considered wise;
when he closes his lips, he is deemed intelligent.

—*Proverbs 17:28*

FASTEN YOUR SEAT BELTS!

When I told my wife what I was going to call this chapter, she said, "Justin, only an extrovert like you can make silence a *festival*." That may be true, but I believe there is so much truth to this concept. My counterparts, the introverts, don't need an exciting term to make them desire silence in their lives because they love it for what it is. But for those of you who are like me, we need to find an exciting motivation to be quiet, and that's why I'm calling it a festival.

In the silence, God stirs in our hearts new ideas, new hopes, new dreams, new ways to love our families. As we listen to him, he inspires questions to ask ourselves. The festival of silence can be compared to riding a roller coaster: Some people get the fast pass and don't have to wait in line, and the excitement comes quicker. Introverts, God bless you! But extroverts like me are more like the two-hour line that I waited in at Cedar Point. We may have to wait a day, a week, or even a month, but God *will* answer. That's when you get to ride the roller coaster. The anticipation of hearing God's voice is the waiting in line part, and when he finally speaks, that's when the ride begins.

But who likes to wait in line? No one! And if you end up getting in the line, odds are that you're only doing so because you think it's going to be amazing. How excited are you to get on the prayer ride? Is it a big deal to hear the voice of God or not? The struggle of waiting and listening in prayer is often stressful and can even be frustrating. But that is a good thing, because it makes hearing God's quiet voice within you all the better when it finally happens. You see, with Christ, tension provides grace. But without Christ, it only provides anger. That tension you feel during or before prayer is an opportunity for God's grace to act freely in you, but it comes with a price. Christ taught that pain and suffering leads to joy. No cross, no crown. No death, no resurrection. No struggle in prayer, no joy of hearing God's voice.

All of our activities, projects, and duties become dry and stale without silence. Silence gives our hearts the time and space to become alive, and that is when we begin to truly live. When we don't take the time to be silent, everything becomes mundane. I sit in silence and ask God, "What do you want me to do today?" And he always gives me something new. If we don't let go of our schedules and activities and make time to get away as Jesus did, even things that used to be exciting to us will become dull. This is because we aren't taking the time to unpack them and discover the depth of each of our experiences that is waiting to be revealed to us.

When I sit down and listen silently to God, he stirs my heart with ideas, such as: "You need to start a 'You're Amazing' crusade! In cities! Go from town to town!" When he fills my heart in prayer with something new, he creates great excitement within me.

Often when I pray in silence, I hear God telling me to ask someone a question. Once, out of the blue, he impressed upon me to ask one of my team members if she was called to be a nun. The anticipation, the excitement of asking that question and wondering if what God put in my heart was real built a festival of anticipation within me like nothing else.

WAIT IN LINE

Nine times out of ten, when it comes to prayer, we'll be waiting in line rather than riding the roller coaster. That period of waiting is often a period of desolation. In a great talk during our missionary training this year, Father Peter Cameron outlined these points about desolation:

- It strives to kill our trust.
- It makes us self-focused, not God focused.
- It makes us feel negative about ourselves and others.
- It causes us to isolate ourselves.

- It makes us uninterested in things that used to be important to us.
- It takes over our thoughts and causes us not to focus on heavenly things.
- It fatigues us and drains us mentally, emotionally, and even physically.

Fr. Peter then talked about what happens during consolation (riding the roller coaster):

- God is showing himself to us clearly during this time.
- It is clear that God is using us in powerful ways.
- It directs us to focus on God.
- It helps us focus on other people's lives.
- It makes us desire to be a part of the community around us.
- It gives us new ideas and inspires us to bring others to Christ.
- It gives us inner peace and refreshes us with new energy.

It is important to be aware of which state you are in. This way, you will know that if you are in desolation, then consolation is on its way, so you won't be tempted to give up before it arrives. If you are in a period of consolation, use it as a time to prepare for the desolation that is to come. God allows those who he knows will come back to him to experience desolation so that we can get stronger. When it doesn't feel like he is present, be assured that it is only because he knows that you will come back to him and that you are committed to him. The more we grow in our faith and in relationship with Jesus, the more desolation we might experience. The spiritual life is an ebb and flow between waiting in line and riding the roller coaster. Buckle up and keep all of your limbs in the cart, because the interior life is one crazy ride!

💡 **QUOTE TO REMEMBER:** "In the silence of the heart God speaks. If you face God in prayer and silence, God will speak to you. Then you will know that you are nothing. It is only when you realize your nothingness, your emptiness, that God can fill you with himself. Souls of prayer are souls of great silence." —Mother Teresa, *In the Heart of the World*

✝ **TIME FOR GOD:** Say this prayer from the Bible every day before your silent time this week: "Speak, Lord, for your servant hears" (1 Samuel 3:9).

🎯 **MAKE IT COUNT:** What state are you in these days? Are you experiencing symptoms of desolation? If so, have faith that a time of consolation is right around the corner.

OUR LIFE IS OUR PRAYER

Pray constantly.

—1 Thessalonians 5:17

In order to offer our entire lives as a prayer, it's important to keep a heavenly focus throughout the day. It's easy to go about our daily tasks and get caught up in a routine, but just as nuns and monks strive for, our work should become our prayer, and our prayer should become our work—they should be one and the same. When our life becomes a prayer, we live in the light and cast away all that is dark.

As with any worthwhile endeavor in life, whether sports, business, or raising a family, goal setting is important to give us guidance. If getting to heaven is our number one goal, then accomplishing that goal is the ultimate fulfillment. St. Paul advised, "Seek the things that are above, where Christ is seated at the right hand of God. Set your minds on things that are above, not on things that are on earth" (Colossians 3:2).

PAIN AND SUFFERING LEAD TO JOY

A few years ago I was really struggling with the prayer we pray five times a day as a team. It goes like this: "Lord Jesus, I give you my life, through pain, through suffering, and through joy." I've prayed this prayer for years, and it has helped me through some very difficult times.

I was struggling with this prayer because it has two parts on the struggles of life and only one part on joy. Everywhere I go, I see pain and suffering, and it was starting to discourage me—this world is a mess! So I brought this to my spiritual director, Fr. Peter Cameron. I explained to him that the focus of the prayer was too much on pain and suffering. Fr. Peter replied in a meek yet confident tone, "Why don't you do an experiment: Tell your missionary team that your spiritual director said they need to change the Hard as Nails prayer. Ask them which part of the prayer they should take out: pain, suffering, or joy? Then see how they respond."

On a bus tour soon after this I said to our team, "I spoke with Fr. Peter last week and he thinks we need to change the Hard as Nails prayer. Which part of the prayer should we take out—pain, suffering, or joy? We are going to take a vote."

They stared at me blankly at first, but soon one missionary piped up and said, "Well . . . Justin, we can't take out suffering."

"Why not?"

"Well, because my dad's in jail. Suffering is what brought me to love Jesus. If I didn't go through that, I'd be just like my dad. If we take out the part about suffering, it's like saying that what we've been through doesn't matter!"

Another missionary jumped in. He began to cry as he said, "We can't take out pain. I thought it was normal to not have a dad until I came here and saw all these people with families. The pain and suffering I went through, even though I didn't totally understand it, is what shaped me into the man I am today.

Someone else said, "What about the thousands of people we meet each year who share about what they went through? We have to let them know that it is going to turn into joy!"

That was all I needed to hear. I took this story back to Fr. Peter, and he said with a smile, "Well, it looks like you'll have to keep the prayer the way it is."

So remember, if your life is full of pain and suffering, keep praying through the challenges. Too many of us think the only time we can pray is when we're sitting in a church. But we can pray in the midst of our daily lives through pain, suffering, and joy. The next time life offers you a trial or a blessing, thank God for it in that moment, and your life will become a prayer.

QUOTE TO REMEMBER: "It is simply impossible to lead, without the aid of prayer, a virtuous life." —St. John Chrysostom

TIME FOR GOD: Reach out to someone who you know prays every day (maybe a grandparent, a parent, a mentor, or a priest). Ask if you can take him or her out to lunch to talk about ways that you can make prayer a part of your everyday life.

MAKE IT COUNT: Commit to three ways to pray that you and this person came up with. Keep him or her updated on how it's going.

OUR LADY IS UNDERRATED

For he has regarded the low estate of his handmaiden. For behold, henceforth all generations will call me blessed.

—Luke 1:48

THE SECRET SAUCE

When I first had my conversion, I prayed the Rosary almost daily. But as time went on, I began to pray it only weekly or monthly. Almost ten years later I met someone at one of my speaking events who asked me if I had consecrated myself to Jesus through Mary. I had no idea what he was talking about. He gave me two books on the subject. A year later I saw him at the same event, and he gave me the books again because I hadn't done it. The third year, he said, "Hey, you're that speaker! Have you done the consecration yet?" I finally decided to do it because, honestly, I felt bad that he had given me six books by this point!

So, in the summer of 2010, my wife and I decided to consecrate our family to Jesus through Mary. When I finally read one of the books, I really liked it because—call me a pagan—you only had to pray a *decade* of the Rosary every day! This seemed doable. I have to admit, even though I had been a Catholic preacher for thirteen years, to me, the Rosary was *boring*!

It wasn't until 2013, when our family began praying a daily Rosary together, that I realized the power of Our Lady. I looked at my wife and asked her, "Why are all these beautiful things happening for our family and the ministry?" That's when I realized how underrated Mary is. My wife told me to ask everyone involved in our mission if they were devoted to Mary. She was right—they were! I can honestly say that it is Our Lady who brings each and every person to our mission. She's the secret sauce!

GIVE HIM A BREAK

During that time, one morning I got up for my silent festival, and I said to God, "Thank you so much for what you've done for my family and this ministry—but why are all these great things happening?" I looked up at our statue of Mary, and in my heart I heard her say, "I went to Jesus for you and told him to give you a break." That touched my heart so deeply!

As I prayed, I realized that it was because of our consecration to Jesus through Mary that my relationship with my wife was growing in such beautiful ways: We had launched our missionary program, I'd found a devoted spiritual director, and Bishop Frank J. Caggiano had become our episcopal adviser for our ministry. After reading *True Devotion to Mary*, by St. Louis de Montfort, Pope John Paul II said, "The reading of this book . . . was a decisive turning point in my life. I say 'turning point,' but in fact it was a long inner journey. . . . This 'perfect devotion' is indispensable to anyone who means to give himself without reserve to Christ and to the work of redemption."

When you make a consecration to Our Lady, the Holy Spirit is able to move more freely in you, and you become more courageous and bold in your faith. In the past, you might have been able to make an impact on others in small ways through your words, but once you are consecrated to Our Lady, the impact is much greater. Your prayer life also becomes more alive and free-flowing.

QUOTE TO REMEMBER: "Never be afraid of loving the Blessed Virgin too much. You can never love her more than Jesus did." —St. Maximilian Kolbe

TIME FOR GOD: Pray a Hail Mary in thanksgiving for those who have helped you in your walk with Christ.

MAKE IT COUNT: Look deeper into doing a family consecration to Jesus through Mary. It will change your life forever.

MERCY WINS

"Go and learn the meaning of the words, 'I desire
mercy, not sacrifice.' I did not come to call
the righteous but sinners."

—*Matthew 9:13*

Often we ignore the most important line in the Our Father: "Forgive us our trespasses as we forgive those who trespass against us." We think we deserve mercy because we are sorry. But the truth is that none of us deserve mercy; it is a free gift from our loving heavenly Father. The only way we can receive this gift is by giving it to others. If we are not willing to show mercy toward those who have hurt us, our hearts do not truly understand its meaning.

MERCY MAKES NO SENSE

One of our missionaries had a cousin who got hit by a car and died when she was nineteen. The man who hit her was her ex-boyfriend, but they were still friends. He'd had one beer. The girl's parents went to his court hearing and said that he shouldn't go to jail—that he should be shown mercy. The judge ruled that since there was alcohol and a death involved, he had to serve time in prison, but he was given the minimum sentence. The ex-boyfriend broke down in tears when the girl's parents spoke up on his behalf.

Those parents knew the meaning of mercy. To the world, what they did seems implausible—and to some, downright wrong. But they knew the words of the Our Father were true, and I believe that God will show them mercy one day because of the choice they made.

YOU TAKE CARE OF IT, DAD

Letting mercy win means leaving justice up to God the Father. If we are so concerned with others getting the judgment we think they deserve, we will never truly understand the meaning of mercy. Mercy is always a clean slate, always a chance to begin again, and always a path to the Father's love. Mercy wins, because it is through mercy that we have salvation. Jesus did not fight back when the soldiers were beating and mocking him. He did not argue with them when they were taunting him on the cross. He simply left it to his heavenly Father to fight the battle, saying, "Father, forgive them; for they know not what they do" (Luke 23:34). To live a life of fulfillment, we too choose to allow mercy to win and leave the judgment to God.

EVERYONE NEEDS MERCY

How can we be merciful? How can we forgive when someone wrongs us? How can we join the ranks of the saints and be merciful to those who have discouraged us, wronged us, and left us in the dust when they were the ones who truly deserved to be miserable and lonely? There is only one way: understanding and knowing in our hearts that someone has had mercy on us. We win, and mercy wins, when we realize that we have been forgiven totally and fully. We will not judge or wrong others when we truly have been at the foot of the cross telling Jesus we're sorry for all we did wrong. We will understand mercy when he looks at us with love and says, "Father, forgive them; for they know not what they do." When we know how merciful Jesus is, then we will extend mercy to others. I know that if I hadn't received mercy for all my sins, I would be far down a different and pretty rough path. Mercy wins when we realize it is not others who need mercy first—we do.

QUOTE TO REMEMBER: "I think we too are the people who, on the one hand want to listen to Jesus, but on the other hand, at times, like to find a stick to beat others with, to condemn others. And Jesus has this message for us: mercy." —Pope Francis

TIME FOR GOD: Pray a divine mercy chaplet and ask God to have mercy on you and the whole world (see http://www.the-divinemercy.org/message/devotions/praythechaplet.php).

MAKE IT COUNT: Go out of your way today to show kindness and mercy toward someone you care about, and expect nothing in return. Make that person's day a little easier by taking something off his or her plate. Help this individual in a small way and make a big impact. A life of fulfillment is often found in the little things.

PASSION

When he saw the crowds, he had compassion for them,
because they were harassed and helpless,
like sheep without a shepherd.

—*Matthew 9:36*

Passion comes from the heart. Our holiness isn't dependent upon how smart we are, but on how passionately we love. We have the capacity to love others like Christ primarily because of our hearts, not our heads. On his deathbed, one of the Catholic Church's greatest theologians, St. Thomas Aquinas, said simply of all that he had learned, "All is straw." At the end of your life, when you are on your deathbed, what you know is not going to matter; how you've formed your heart to love God and his people will.

Our hearts are the home for God, and that is what makes us amazing. At times our thoughts, feelings, and emotions will tempt and even lead us away from the reality of our amazingness.

We will hear, and sometimes believe, the lies of the enemy—lies that tell us we are no good, that we should seek what we want for ourselves above all else, that we should give in to our temptations, that we don't need to pray, that we know better than God. These lies, when entertained over time, can create a hardness in our hearts. This hardness does not change the essence of our amazing hearts, but it can create a distortion in us that makes it challenging to believe in God's goodness, our own goodness, and the goodness of others.

This battle will rage throughout our lives, but we have some mighty weapons at our disposal. The Bible says in Matthew 6:21, "For where your treasure is, there will your heart be also." The victory is ours in Christ. If we want our hearts to be a place for God, we have to focus our time and thoughts on the things of God. We have to do what we can to make him our treasure. His Word will direct our paths; it will help us to discipline ourselves in our moral choices and recognize our nothingness without him. We will be led to pray more, and we will experience an increase in our yearning for God in our lives.

This is in stark contrast to the fruit of our negative thoughts and actions. When we form negative habits that change our hearts from what they were meant to be, we end up replacing what is meant for God with sinful desires that can never satisfy. If we form our hearts to love money, then we continually discipline and develop our hearts to desire money. If we form our hearts to be impure, we end up developing and cultivating impure thoughts and relationships. But if we form our hearts to desire true fulfillment, then we will continually work hard and focus our energy, our minds, our feelings, our emotions, and our intuitions on finding the truth. What do you think about the most? That's your treasure. That's your heart.

Truth is the cornerstone of our heart, but sometimes the truth can hurt, so we run from it. Feelings and emotions can be good, but they can also lead us astray. Truth is what will lead us to Christ. If we have formed our hearts to be in line with truth, then they will become a place of encounter with the Lord. The *Catechism of the Catholic Church* says:

> The heart is our hidden center, beyond the grasp of our reason and of others; only the Spirit of God can fathom the human heart and know it fully. The heart is the place of decision, deeper than our psychic drives. It is the place of truth, where we choose life or death. It is the place of encounter, because as image of God we live in relation: it is the place of covenant. (*CCC*, 2563)

If someone takes illegal drugs, it taints his heart, but the amazingness in his heart doesn't change. The mind is impacted negatively by that drug, but the heart is not destroyed at all. When someone decides as a little kid to hurt others because she has been hurt by an adult, this affects her emotions and feelings toward others and herself, but it does not affect her heart. When people take illegal drugs, or lash out at others because someone has lashed out at them, a crust forms around their hearts and prevents them from being the people God intended them to be. It doesn't destroy their amazing hearts, though.

We are made for God; therefore our hearts always long for him. We can mistake that longing for him for a longing for temporary or even sinful things, however. Pay attention to what your heart is telling you in any given situation or relationship. Once your heart is conformed to the will of God, if something is not meant to be, your heart will say, "It doesn't fit." You can always trust your heart to bring you to the truth when you have formed it to desire God.

Many people think that only our minds matter. It is important to develop our minds, but they are nothing without the vital piece—our hearts. Blessed Basil Moreau, founder of the Congregation of Holy Cross, said in his book *Christian Education*, "How we educate the mind will change with the times; how we cultivate the heart is and will remain timeless." When your heart is formed with a good, noble conscience, look for God's amazing plan for your life to unfold.

QUOTE TO REMEMBER: "Education of the mind without education of the heart is no education at all." —Aristotle

TIME FOR GOD: Ask someone who is going through a struggle if you can be there for him or her during this tough time. Pray that God gives you the right words to say, and don't be afraid to pray out loud with that person.

MAKE IT COUNT: Think of some ways you can increase your passion and strengthen your heart. Then get ready for God to show you how amazing you are.

JOIN THE BREAKFAST CLUB

Are not those who eat the sacrifices
participants in the altar?

—*1 Corinthians 10:18*

YOU'RE BORING

We've all been caught being bored at Mass at times, but if the celebration of the Eucharist shared there has been preserved for more than two thousand years and is the "source and summit" of our Catholic faith (*CCC*, 1324), then there must be something to it. I always say, "If you think Mass is boring, then *you're* boring! When I first had my conversion, I got so excited about getting to Mass and so annoyed that there were only two others with me that I started literally headlocking kids into Mass. I don't suggest you do the same, but my hope is that you're just as enthusiastic about getting others there. The real breakfast of champions is the Eucharist.

We think Mass is boring because we are going into it looking to get something out of it for ourselves. Mass is boring when it's about me, me, me. When I realized that it's about Christ and not about me, then I started to get something out of it because I knew that God had the grace that I needed to deal with daily struggles and annoyances right there waiting for me. Although that grace helps me in my daily life, it has nothing to do with me. The grace is Christ *in* me.

I'M FULL!

Everyone loves food. I'm not just saying that because I am Italian and my mom is a great cook. Anyone who does not like food has something seriously wrong with them. I mean, *seriously*. When it comes down to it, we all need food to keep us alive. It gives us the nourishment and energy we require to get through the day. Think about every significant gathering of your family and friends—holidays, funerals, weddings, birthdays, picnics. They all have one thing in common: food! Food brings people together around the table. That's why God chose to give us a meal in the Mass, so we can gather around his table and feast with him.

When we worship God, we empty ourselves and make room for the fulfillment of life itself—Jesus Christ. When we receive the Eucharist at Mass and we listen to the Word of God and let it penetrate our hearts, we are fulfilled because God injects us with his love, joy, truth, and peace and he rids us of the lies of sinfulness, discouragement, and shame.

The Mass has to be more than just Catholic calisthenics— and it is. In the Mass, God invites us to come together and remember how much he loves us. It's kind of like those family gatherings where there are all sorts of characters present. We love them no matter how insane they might be because they are our family. That is what the Mass is supposed to do: welcome *everyone* in, with no one excluded, so everyone can celebrate and remember God together and be nourished by that heavenly food.

I once heard a priest say that if he was at the front of a church handing out one million dollars to each person in the Communion line, there would be much better attendance. But in the Eucharist, we get so much more. We get to draw closer to God and feast, feast, feast!

START YOUR OWN BREAKFAST CLUB

A Breakfast Club is so simple, anyone can start one. All it takes is a priest to say Mass and someone to provide some food afterward. Then you invite all your friends and the people you meet to come to the Breakfast Club after Mass, and after you get your heavenly food with your community, you share your earthly food with them. Let's be honest—food gets people in the door. God kept the Israelites moving through the desert by giving them quail and manna every night and morning, and just enough for one serving each so they couldn't store it up. Watch your community grow in zeal, prayerfulness, and unity by starting a Breakfast Club today.

💡 **QUOTE TO REMEMBER:** "The Mass is very long and tiresome unless one loves God." —G. K. Chesterton

✝ **TIME FOR GOD:** Make time in your schedule to go to daily Mass during the week. Note in your journal what God speaks to you during Mass from now on. (You can request a free Mass journal from DynamicCatholic.com.)

◎ **MAKE IT COUNT:** Go to daily Mass once a month and invite someone who is there to go to breakfast with you and your friends afterward, even if you get rejected. You might start a new tradition!

PART IV
Be Humble

START AT ZERO

The steadfast love of the Lord never ceases, his mercies never come to an end; they are new every morning; great is your faithfulness.

—Lamentations 3:22–23

Yesterday is over, and if we think of all the horrible or great things we did yesterday, we will miss out on what we are called to do today. Along the way in this life, we will experience rejection, hurt, and misunderstanding as well as joy, excitement, and contentment. Yet every day is a fresh page, a clean start. We need to start at zero every day. Jesus knew some days would be better than others. Let's take a look at some of his greatest preaching of all time, the Beatitudes (Matthew 5:3-10), to see what we have to look forward to after all this suffering on earth.

THE BEATITUDES

Blessed are the poor in spirit,
for theirs is the kingdom of heaven.

Blessed are they who mourn,
for they shall be comforted.

Blessed are the meek,
for they shall inherit the earth.

Blessed are they who hunger and thirst for righteousness,
for they shall be satisfied.

Blessed are the merciful,
for they shall obtain mercy.

Blessed are the pure of heart,
for they shall see God.

Blessed are the peacemakers,
for they shall be called children of God.

Blessed are they who are persecuted for the sake of righteousness,
for theirs is the kingdom of heaven.

In a nutshell, the way I see it, Jesus' greatest preaching says, "Please go out and fail." This is a foreign concept in the success-driven world that we live in. The second line in each beatitude describes what heaven will look like *if* we follow the first line. Jesus knows the struggles and trials we'll have on earth, but he wants us to go for it anyway. When we fail we usually feel bad, but God wants us to know that we can fail forward.

At the risk of sounding heretical, I've rewritten the Beatitudes from the point of view of a typical success-driven American. The outcome of living the Beatitudes if you have a worldly perspective, a perspective in which heaven does *not* exist, is pure failure and disgrace. Take a look:

THE WORLDLY BEATITUDES

Blessed are the poor in spirit,
For they are a bunch of whiners.

Blessed are they who mourn,
For their friends will die and they'll never see them again.

Blessed are they who hunger and thirst for righteousness,
For they will be called bigots.

Blessed are the merciful,
For they will be run over and taken advantage of.

Blessed are the pure of heart,
For they are missing out on lots of exciting things.

Blessed are the peacemakers,
For their life is really boring.

Blessed are they who are persecuted for the sake of righteousness,
For they are rejected and a bunch of nerds.

We know that because we have an eternal perspective, our reward will be great in heaven . . . and no, we won't be a bunch of losers in eternity—we will be fulfilled! The Beatitudes are meant to be guidelines for those who are seeking eternal Truth, not temporary acceptance or success. People who live only for this world cannot understand the power of the Beatitudes. In the world's view, we need prizes and constant encouragement to pump up our self-esteem, and we want most people, if not all, to like and appreciate us. But in God's view, none of that matters. In the world's view, it's all about how we are treated. In God's view, it is knowing there is a greater purpose in life than the reactions of others. When we live out the Beatitudes, our faith, hope, confidence, and trust in God becomes the power that carries us through the times we have been wrongly called whiners, bigots, boring, or a nuisance, or when someone shouts at us, "There is no heaven, so cut the Jesus stuff!"

The word *blessed* means "happy," and true happiness comes from knowing God and living for him. Our humble identity comes from knowing how little we are and how big God is. He has already handled all of the problems and challenges that we will ever face. When we understand this, we will have peace, comfort, mercy, and fulfillment—in other words, an amazing life. If we do our best to follow God, and start at zero every day, he will take care of the results, whether we see them or not.

QUOTE TO REMEMBER: "Place yourself before God in your helplessness; consent to the fact that you are powerless to slay yourself; give yourself in patient and trustful surrender to God. Accept every humiliation; look upon every person who tries or troubles you as a means of grace to humble you." —Andrew Murray

TIME FOR GOD: Pray with the Beatitudes, and insert your name, saying "Blessed is _____."

Imagine yourself in heaven—what will eternal life be like?

MAKE IT COUNT: Pick the beatitude that is hardest for you to live out, and focus on it every day for one week. Fulfillment means working toward your goal every day.

SIGNIFICANCE OVER SUCCESS

I praise you, for I am wondrously made. Wonderful are your works! You know me right well.

—Psalm 139:14

KEEP YOUR EYES OPEN

We're told that we should focus on the success we're striving for, but we often forget about the people right in front of us. What matters most is how we treat the person who needs us the most in any given moment, not whether or not we get a task done. The truth is that God is going to judge us not by our successes but by how we treat those around us while we are on the way to those successes. Whenever I see the maintenance man who works the grounds at our office, I usually just say a simple hello. One day, I decided to stop and ask him how he was doing because I knew his mother had just passed away. I walked back into the office after forty-five minutes of listening to his heart. One of the staff members said, "I saw your van pull up a while ago—what were you doing out there talking to the maintenance man?" I was convicted in that moment, and thought, *It's time to put the success down and focus on being significant to others.* We are too busy running around like chickens with our heads cut off most of the time to see the person right in front of us who might be struggling and in need of our encouragement.

That day after I spoke to the maintenance man, I forgot my phone charger in the van, so I hurried back out of the office and ran into a man I often see sitting in the back of the church at daily Mass. God was giving me another opportunity to listen to a suffering soul. I invited him to come out to lunch with me and some of our staff members. We sat at Panda Express for more than two hours as he shared his heart.

Most of us do not realize how amazing we truly are. That day I found out how amazing my daily Mass friend was. He told us how his wife had divorced him, stolen tens of thousands of dollars from him, and had been cheating on him for years. Holy cow! None of us had any idea how much of a struggle he had been going through. He shared how hurt he was and how much suffering he and his daughters were going through.

I asked him one simple question: "What has helped you through it?"

He told me, "I prayed constantly . . . twenty-*five* hours a day!" He looked at me with tears in his eyes and continued, "Justin, it was when the missionaries from your mission came and prayed with me that I decided to start moving forward again in my life." He is on the road to healing and forgiveness because a few young people were present to him.

True humility is knowing how amazing God made us. We need to remember that it is not about what we *do*, but who we *are*—we are all amazing! When we know we are amazing, we will focus on being significant to others. With humility we spread the message to others that they are amazing, just like we are, but in their own, unique ways.

IT'S ABOUT *WHO* YOU ARE

You see, our success in life will vary over time, but our significance will never change. For each one of us, young or old, missionary or business leader, our significance comes from being present to others and listening to their sacred stories. That daily Mass friend changed my life that day. He made me realize the "You're Amazing" message: People don't matter because they've sinned less or more. It's not important whether they play in the NFL, win the Nobel Peace Prize, or are even in jail. People matter and are significant because of who we are to them, and who they are to us—dad, friend, grandmother, encourager.

When Jesus said, "No longer do I call you servants . . . but I have called you friends" (John 15:15), he was really saying, "When you were a servant, you thought I cared about what you did or didn't do for me. But now that you know that you are my friend, what matters most is that you are significant to me and my Father in heaven. You are my friend because we have failed together and succeeded together. We have struggled, and we have conquered. What matters most of all is that we spend time together."

Being truly humble means knowing that *everyone* is amazing. Some people look at others and say, "They don't seem amazing!" But I say, "They are someone's friend. They are someone's brother. They may seem like a failure to us, but they are surely significant to someone else." You could lose your job, your status, or your money, but your love and care for one another cannot be taken away. No matter what you do in life, you can always love and you can always listen. We need to keep our eyes fixed on being significant and focus less on being successful.

💡 **QUOTE TO REMEMBER:** "A life isn't significant except for its impact on other lives." —Jackie Robinson

✝ **TIME FOR GOD:** Pray the Prayer of Abandonment:

> *Father, I abandon myself into your hands;*
> *do with me what you will.*
> *Whatever you may do, I thank you:*
> *I am ready for all, I accept all.*
> *Let only your will be done in me, and in all your creatures—*
> *I wish no more than this, O Lord.*
> *Into your hands I commend my soul:*
> *I offer it to you with all the love of my heart,*
> *for I love you, Lord, and so need to give myself,*
> *to surrender myself into your hands without reserve,*

and with boundless confidence,
for you are my Father.

MAKE IT COUNT: Write a letter out of the blue to someone you care about, telling this individual how amazing you think he or she is. Work toward being significant in that person's life.

IT'S NOT ABOUT ME— IT'S ABOUT WE

Truly, truly, I say to you, he who believes in me will also do the works that I do; and greater works than these will he do, because I go to the Father.

—John 14:12

Why did Jesus decide to have twelve apostles? Why did he need a team? And why on earth did he choose a bunch of sinners?

All of us work together with many different teams, whether in sports, schools, church, or at work. Jesus gave us one of the greatest lessons in life: A team does not need to be perfect to do great things. Teamwork requires working through challenges together with a group of imperfect people, being willing to struggle, fail, fight, question, or make impulsive decisions. But with Jesus at the helm, all of this leads to a great outcome.

Jesus knew that even though he could bring God's message to the world by himself, his Father wanted him to work as a team with the apostles. We need to work as a team too. Especially today, many of us are inclined to have a Lone Ranger mentality. We might think, *I can do this on my own,* or we might go to the other extreme and think, *Nobody needs me.* Jesus knew that the team approach was the winning approach. It's important for us to learn that even though teamwork can be difficult, it is more rewarding than going solo; there is more energy to give and more can be accomplished for the kingdom of God. Most people would think that accomplishing a task on your own would be more fulfilling. But if you've ever accomplished something because every member of your team played a crucial part in the success, you know that "the more, the merrier" applies here. An accomplishment with a team is much more rewarding than success on your own, because you are humbled enough to know you couldn't do it on your own.

In my own life, while I have certainly struggled with being part of a team, I have learned how hard it is to make a significant impact on the world around me without one. Some of us have encountered teammates who have backstabbed us. Jesus knew which of the apostles would be the backstabber, yet he still decided he wanted him on his team. Other members of Jesus' team struggled with anger, fought for power, did not trust him, did not listen to him, doubted him, and even denied him; sometimes we will have team members like that too.

But I believe that in order to develop a deeper relationship with God, we must build a team around us like Jesus did—

which sometimes takes a lot of humility. Being on a team shows us that it is not all about *us*; it's about what we can do *together*. When Jesus formed his team of twelve, he sent them two by two from town to town. He empowered his team and gave them the ability to do even greater things than he would during his time on earth.

Building a team hurts because love hurts. It is hard to watch our best friends make mistakes. It hurts when someone gives up on life. Our family is the most important team we will ever be on, but it is also the hardest team to be on. Jesus' family was the team that was there for him when he faced his greatest suffering on the cross. In the same way, our family is meant to be there for us when we face our own crosses, and vice versa. Our teammates can pick us up when we are down, they can remind us who we are when we're tempted to forget, and together we can do much more than we ever dreamed we could do on our own. If I had not built a team around me, the "You're Amazing" message would not be thriving today. I can't even imagine where we would be if I did not have my wife, staff, missionary team, and the many donors, volunteers, guides, and friends of the ministry. God humbled me and showed me that teamwork is the greatest way to go. What I am lacking in gifts or skills, the others on the team make up for.

Two of the most important questions you can ask yourself are: "Do I have a team?" and "Am I on Jesus' team?" Remember, teamwork makes the dream work. You will realize your dreams only with the help of the amazing people you have on your team.

QUOTE TO REMEMBER: "Alone we can do so little; together we can do so much." —Helen Keller

TIME FOR GOD: Take an hour in a church (in front of the Blessed Sacrament, if you can), and pray about whether or not you are on Jesus' team. Be honest with yourself and with God about where you are in your faith. If you are not on Jesus' team, what do you need to change?

MAKE IT COUNT: Who are the key players in your life (family, friends, coworkers, those you are reading this book with)? Together go out and help the homeless, those in a nursing home, kids with cancer, etc. Decide to do a project that is about "we," not "me."

LEAD LIKE JESUS

Have this mind among yourselves, which was in Christ
Jesus, who, though he was in the form of God, did not
count equality with God a thing to be grasped, but emp-
tied himself, taking the form of a servant, being born in
the likeness of men. And being found in human form he
humbled himself and became obedient unto death,
even death on a cross

—*Philippians 2:5–8*

WHO BROUGHT ST. TERESA OF CALCUTTA TO JESUS?

My good friend and mentor Ken Blanchard, whom I wrote
about in chapter five, has written many successful books (with
more than twenty million sold, I might add). The one that I
think took the most courage and humility for him to write was
Lead Like Jesus. He wrote this book with one of his best friends,
Phil Hodges. You may have never heard of Phil Hodges, but I bet

you've never heard about the person who changed St. Teresa of Calcutta's life or St. Francis of Assisi's life either. Anyway, Phil Hodges was the one who prayed, encouraged, and taught Ken Blanchard about having a true relationship with Jesus. Leading like Jesus means passing the faith on to others without need of earthly recognition.

When Phil heard about the success of one of Ken's previous books, *The One Minute Manager*, he asked him to take a walk on the beach with him. During that walk, he asked Ken, "Why do you think this book is more successful than the other books you've written?"

Ken said, "Phil, I think somehow *God* was involved."

Phil started sending Ken Christian material to read, but Ken was slow to really engage with it. Then God brought another Christian friend to guide Ken along the way, the great writer and speaker Norman Vincent Peale. Norman said to Ken, "The Lord's always had you on his team—you just haven't suited up yet." And that was the start of a whole new ball game for Ken Blanchard.

When we lead like Jesus, we will surely make an impact on the world, but as with Phil Hodges, people might not even know our names. But Jesus does—guaranteed. *Leading like Jesus means we deny ourselves so that others may do greater things than we will ever do.* We can start by asking ourselves, "How are we going to impact others' lives?" We might never know how much the little things we do, the prayers we pray, or the publications we share mean to the people in our lives, but leading like Jesus is not about doing things so others might see the impact; it's about doing it for Jesus, especially when no one is looking. It's about learning to love with our hearts, our heads, our hands, and our habits. It's about making God a part of everything we do.

JOSEPH'S VOICE

St. Joseph was a man who followed the will of God but did not need to be recognized. There is no record of Joseph saying anything in the Bible, but what a great man he was! He did not need recognition on earth in order to do great things for God. He humbly followed God's guidance, whether from an angel, a dream, or God himself—even when his betrothed got pregnant out of wedlock and by earthly standards he should have had her stoned.

St. Joseph was the foster father of Jesus and raised him as his own son, and yet we do not often hear about him in the Christian life. He must have taught Jesus the Scriptures, how to be a man, and how to work with his hands. God humbled himself and became man, a creature less than himself, subject to the care of other humans. Jesus allowed himself to be raised by parents just like the rest of us. He lived the first thirty years of his life under the radar, just like his earthly father. Joseph cared for and protected his wife and the son God had entrusted to him. He had much he could have boasted about, but he kept his mouth shut and lived with a humble heart. Joseph was one of the best leaders who ever lived, and it wasn't because he told everyone what to do. He was an example of true leadership: He was humble enough to learn from others, and he didn't need to be in the limelight in order to lead others; his character spoke for itself.

💡 **QUOTE TO REMEMBER:** "None of us is as smart as all of us." —Ken Blanchard

✝ **TIME FOR GOD:** Prayerfully read Luke 24:13–35. Notice how Jesus leads his disciples by asking questions. What can you learn from Jesus to help you become a better leader?

🎯 **MAKE IT COUNT:** The next time someone wrongly credits someone else for something you did—let him! Being fulfilled doesn't mean being recognized; it means doing what is right.

THREE MINUTES OF POWER

Always be prepared to make a defense to any one who calls you to account for the hope that is in you, yet do it with gentleness and reverence.

—*1 Peter 3:15–16*

THE POWER OF YOUR STORY

Victor was one of our missionaries and had an amazing message. I remember vividly the poignant moment at a men's conference when he shared how devastated he was when his mother died. He knew he needed to let go of his hatred and all-consuming anger, and just before she died, his mother advised him to do exactly that. She said, "Victor, do not be angry with God; go to him with everything." Although he had wrestled with these negative emotions for years, he was now ready to openly forgive God and many others in his life, especially his father.

I asked the men in the audience, "How many of you need to forgive someone? How many of you need to let go of some hurt you may have been holding on to for years?" Out of the corner of my eye, I saw an elderly man slowly making his way toward Victor—he had to be at least ninety years old. That man looked up at Victor with tears in his eyes, hugged him, and whispered, "I need to forgive my dad too. God bless you, son." That man (let's be real) was going to meet Jesus soon, and he was able to be set free before he left this earth.

Now it's your turn. The most important question to ask yourself is: "Am I determined and humble enough to let myself be set free from my addictions, past hurts, attitude problems, or whatever has held me back? Am I ready to be real and go to Jesus with my whole heart?" Jesus wants to take your burdens. Give God all your heavy baggage, and he will carry it for you.

THE THREE MINUTES OF POWER

I frequently use something I call the Three Minutes of Power. It's similar to an elevator speech—a clear, concise "commercial" about you, your product, or your business. An elevator speech communicates who you are, what you're looking for, and how you can benefit an individual or a company. The Three Minutes of Power communicates the power of Jesus Christ in a concise, compelling way. If you only had three minutes to help someone get to heaven, what would you say?

The Three Minutes of Power has the potential to change the world. We travel across the country in a large tour bus. Our logo on that bus reads, YOU'RE AMAZING, and underneath it is the phrase A MESSAGE OF HOPE THAT WILL CHANGE YOUR LIFE FOREVER. Fr. Larry taught me that the most important thing we can do is give people a reason for their hope, and that hope is found only in Jesus Christ (he also said that we stole that phrase from him, but God knows the truth!).

Jesus gives us hope that goes far beyond our human understanding, and he won this hope for us on the cross. To the world it sounds crazy that his *death* gives us hope. But when you know Jesus, you understand how powerful the cross is. "The message of the cross is foolishness to those who are perishing, but to us who are being saved it is the power of God" (1 Corinthians 1:18). In heaven we'll have the privilege of meeting all those who have received grace from the power of the cross.

When we share our story with others, they'll hear about a love that never gives up. They'll hear about the freedom and grace Jesus offers. In effect, by sharing our personal story with others, we are sharing Christ and his story.

THE POWER OF THE CROSS

The cross is the most powerful gift that God has given us. It is a paradox, a mystery, and most of all, it is a powerful weapon that can bring all of us together. Through the cross, we realize that suffering is a gift. Our team has been through a lot of tough times, just like you. Some members of the team have been abused by a father, grandfather, or boyfriend. Others have been abandoned by their dads, discouraged by a best friend, bullied, or have even experienced the humiliation of vulnerable pictures of themselves sent over the Internet. There is so much suffering in the world.

Take a good look at a crucifix, and then ask yourself, "Why does a large part of the world's population wear a piece of jewelry with such a horrific image around their necks every day?" Imagine if hundreds of thousands of people around the world wore *your* most mortifying and excruciating suffering depicted on a necklace? That's the kind of love God has for us. The crucifixion, although horrific, calls us to reflect that authentic, selfless love.

Father Mike Schmitz said it best: "God showed us His wounds so that we would not be afraid to show him ours." I would take it one step further and say that God showed us his wounds so we would not be afraid to show Him—and even the whole world—our wounds. We are the body of Christ on earth. Let's carry each other's crosses together. We can start by using the Three Minutes of Power.

HOW TO SHARE YOUR THREE MINUTES

FIRST: Share your "cross"—your greatest challenge (one minute).

SECOND: Share what Jesus has done for you and why you live for him (one minute).

FINALLY: Share what you are grateful for (one minute).

THE RESULT: Your Three Minutes of Power will bring hope to a hurting world.

For the first minute, you share with the world the greatest challenge that you face—the losses you've experienced, the hurts you've endured, the anxiety you feel. This is the hardest minute, but your honesty will empower others to see Jesus in you.

The second minute of power expresses how you've experienced Christ's peace in your life. It could be a small, simple moment—not everyone has a giant *wow* experience. What matters most is that you are sincere and real. It lets others know you haven't always been like this, that it's been a process—and that gives people hope.

The third minute will have an effect on even the hardest of hearts. Someone might be successful in the worldly sense yet suffering inside. This minute lets the person know that we can be grateful regardless of our circumstances. Gratefulness is powerful! Remember, you carry your story with you wherever you go.

💡 **QUOTE TO REMEMBER:** "Tribulation is a gift from God—one that he especially gives his special friends." —St. Thomas More

✝ **TIME FOR GOD:** Ask God the Father to heal you and help you overcome the challenges you face. Pray that he will give you the courage you need to share your story, and pray with gratitude for all you have.

◎ **MAKE IT COUNT:** Make a commitment to share your Three Minutes of Power with someone new at least once a week.

HUMILITY BEARS FRUIT

Whoever exalts himself will be humbled, and whoever humbles himself will be exalted.

—Matthew 23:12

THE HUMILITY SCALE

Being humbled has the potential to bear the greatest fruit in our lives if we can handle it the right way—with humility. In her book *In the Heart of the World*, St. Teresa of Calcutta said:

> Humility is the mother of all virtues. It is in being humble that our love becomes real, devoted, and ardent. If you are humble, nothing will touch you; neither praise, nor disgrace because you know what you are. If you are blamed, you will not be discouraged. If they call you a saint, you will not put yourself on a pedestal.

What Mother Teresa is talking about here is finding a balance. We find our understanding of humility from the Latin word *humus*, which means "of the dirt." The English word *human* also comes from this root, and in this way, we remember that with Adam's creation, we came from the earth, the most grounded position. Humility is not thinking poorly of oneself—God does not make junk! How many of us look in the mirror and think, *I'm not as skinny as I would like to be,* or *I'm nothing; I suck?* St. Leo the Great said during his papacy, "Recognize your dignity, oh Christian!"

On the other end of the spectrum, we can think too highly and too much of ourselves. Some of us look in the mirror and think, *There's no one better than me! I'm the man!* That's not humble either. True humility is knowing who you are in the eyes of God—who does God say you are?

One of our staff members is on the low end of the scale in terms of how she views herself. She knows that her negative thought patterns are not helping her to live a fulfilled life. She deals with these negative thoughts by giving herself a pep talk every morning in front of the mirror. When her mind tells her that she sucks, she looks at her reflection and says, "I'm amazing! I'm the best! I am loved!" She's bumping the gauge *up* on the scale. In a similar way, if you are someone who naturally thinks too highly of yourself, you might bump your scale down by saying something like, "Come on, Jack! You've got work to do! It's time to go out there and start making something of yourself!" The words we use when we think about ourselves can change how humble we are.

Before we work on any of the other virtues, we must consider humility and its counterpart, which is magnanimity. *Magnanimity* is just a big word for "greatness of spirit." It's about seeking greatness in one's life, and this is what God calls us to do every day. Too often we are scared of the call to greatness—we've been trained to be merely mediocre. When we do great things, people will often want to drag us down. But God has great things in store for the one who lets him work. When I was seventeen, I told God I would do anything for him, and when I got to college, some people called me magnanimous in a negative way. They said I was too zealous, but I stayed true to God's call and continued to strive for greatness.

To understand who you truly are, it's important to recognize your lowliness as a human being before God, as well as the greatness of what he calls you to be. We'll never be completely humble, but humility is the most important virtue for us to strive for. We can look to Mary, who was the first follower of Christ; she is the perfect example of humility for us. She was both a handmaid and a queen, and humbly confident in both.

The key to practicing humility is being aware of the broad spectrum of this virtue and its opposing vices, which are pusillanimity (thinking too little of self) and pride (thinking too much of self). In life, people might call you the nicest person on the planet, while the next day others will call you a menace to society. Only in God can you find the truth. As priest and theologian Desiderius Erasmus said, "Humility is truth." Humility is knowing who you really are.

💡 **QUOTE TO REMEMBER:** "If we are humble, we cannot be humiliated." —Fr. Cajetan Mary da Bergamo

✝ **TIME FOR GOD:** Pray the Litany of Humility.

> *O Jesus! meek and humble of heart, hear me.*
> *From the desire of being esteemed,*
> *   Deliver me, Jesus. (repeat after every line)*
> *From the desire of being loved . . .*
> *From the desire of being extolled . . .*
> *From the desire of being honored . . .*
> *From the desire of being praised . . .*
> *From the desire of being preferred to others . . .*
> *From the desire of being consulted . . .*
> *From the desire of being approved . . .*
> *From the fear of being humiliated . . .*
> *From the fear of being despised . . .*
> *From the fear of suffering rebukes . . .*
> *From the fear of being calumniated . . .*
> *From the fear of being forgotten . . .*
> *From the fear of being ridiculed . . .*
> *From the fear of being wronged . . .*
> *From the fear of being suspected . . .*
>
> *That others may be loved more than I,*
> *   Jesus, grant me the grace to desire it. (repeat after every line)*
> *That others may be esteemed more than I . . .*
> *That, in the opinion of the world,*

others may increase and I may decrease . . .

That others may be chosen and I set aside . . .

That others may be praised and I unnoticed . . .

That others may be preferred to me in everything . . .

That others may become holier than I, provided that I may become as holy as I should . . .

MAKE IT COUNT: Who is the most humble person you know? Get your friends together and designate a day when you show your appreciation toward that person. Those who are humble don't often get recognized.

NO PROBLEMS, JUST OPPORTUNITIES

Commit your works to the Lord,
and your plans will be established.

—Proverbs 16:3

Patrick Lencioni, a good friend of mine and one of the best business management leaders out there, once said, "His biggest problem was his need for a problem." Many people seem to seek out problems wherever they go. Without problems, they don't know how to function. If they come across a minor roadblock, they immediately jump to the worst possible conclusion. Not only that, but they bring everyone else into the problem, and soon the whole group believes the world is ending! When I'm around people like this, I'm always amazed at how quickly things escalate. This type of behavior is childish, but aren't we all guilty of it now and then? When we are faced with a difficulty in life, how many of us revert to despair and negativity?

GOD'S PLAN B BEATS OUR PLAN A

Sometimes the "problems" we encounter come when the plans we've made for our lives don't work out. As the saying goes, "If you want to make God laugh, tell him your plans!" Most of us come up with an extensive plan for our life, set goals, and do our best to accomplish them so that we can have the best life possible—a life of fulfillment. Some of us might not plan out our entire life; maybe we tend to focus on our weeks or our days. Either way, we come up with plan A, shooting for the best possible outcome. However, more often than not, these plans turn out completely different than we imagined, and suddenly we realize we need a plan B. (Wait! We didn't plan for this!)

You see, the thing about plan B is that you never see it coming. Plan B is almost always a surprise. It comes out of left field every time. You can't plan for plan B, because it isn't ours to plan. Plan B is an opportunity for God to come through.

God envisioned a perfect plan for our lives (plan A) when he created the world and everything in it. Then Adam and Eve came along and sinned and messed up the whole deal for the rest of us. But what did God end up doing? He did something completely unexpected (here comes plan B, the opportunity). He literally sent his only son to the earth to die for all of humanity so we can live with him for eternity in heaven. Because of Adam and Eve's sin, we get to have eternal life . . . didn't see that coming!

Adam and Eve probably thought that their whole life was going to fall apart. They probably felt hopeless and guilty. They probably felt downright horrible about themselves. But God came through like he always does—with an opportunity. He worked with the evil they brought upon themselves and made a plan B for Adam and Eve, and for all of us too. And guess what—it's actually better than plan A, because plan B gave us Jesus Christ, who is alive in us in an intimate way through the mercy and grace of his crucifixion. As the words of the Easter Vigil proclaim, "O happy fault, that gained for us so great a Redeemer."

So the next time your plan A falls apart, the next time your hope is lost, the next time you feel like your whole life is crashing down—hold on tight, because God is waiting to surprise you with the opportunity of plan B, and you might not even see it coming.

All throughout salvation history, God has taken what we see as problems and used them as opportunities. He started with Adam and Eve and continued to do the same with Noah, Moses, Joshua, Gideon, Deborah, Elijah, Job—all the way to you and me!

THE REMEDY

If you honestly reflect on your own life, can you see how the Lord has taken your plan A and turned it into a plan B? Can you see how he took your problem and turned it into an opportunity? Have you been hurt by a friend? Maybe God taught you to trust him more. Have you had to beat an addiction in your life? Maybe through this, he taught you that you are capable of much more than you ever thought possible.

Two ways to overcome the problems in our lives and let God turn them into opportunities are by being *hopeful* and by being *grateful*. Being hopeful means learning from the past and not letting our past dictate our future. When we are grateful, we are able to trust in God's plan, whether that's plan A or plan B. When we trust in the Lord and are grateful for the life he's given us, there is nothing to worry about, and there are no problems.

💡 **QUOTE TO REMEMBER:** "Pray, hope, and don't worry."
—St. Pio of Pietrelcina

✝ **TIME FOR GOD:** Pray the Serenity Prayer today:

> *God, grant me the serenity to accept the things I cannot change,*
> *Courage to change the things I can,*
> *And wisdom to know the difference.*

Ask God to show you what are the things that you cannot change and what are the things that you can change. Surrender those things to him today.

🎯 **MAKE IT COUNT:** Make two columns in your journal:

> Column 1: Problems you've faced in life
> Column 2: Opportunities that came from each of those
>   problems

Then thank God for giving you what you needed in each situation. Fulfillment means forming an attitude of gratitude.

GRATEFULNESS

*O how abundant is your goodness, which you have laid
up for those who fear you, and wrought for
those who take refuge in you!*

—Psalm 31:20

YOU HAVE EVERYTHING YOU NEED

Society tells us that everyone in the family is entitled to a cell phone, a house, and a car. It's considered the norm to be guaranteed three meals a day and unlimited snacks at our disposal, to have a mom and a dad, a grandpa and a grandma, and friends around us who love us no matter what. But by taking a careful look around, we learn that many of us don't have these things.

The first time I lost someone I loved was when I was twelve years old. My Nooker, my Italian grandfather, died. I was so sad and could not understand why he had to die. I remember going to his funeral and hearing people talk about what an amazing man my grandfather was and how they were so grateful for him. Through this I realized that even though my Nooker died, I can be grateful for the time I had him in my life and the legacy he left.

Having humility of heart means truly understanding that not everyone has a grandpa, or a dad, or even enough food on the table. We have all been given our own challenges for a particular reason, and none of us are entitled to what we have been given. The only reason we have anything is because we have a God who loves us. Being thankful to God for all the gifts that he gives us keeps us humble, because we know we must rely on him for all things. In the Old Testament, the word *poverty* translates as "spiritual dependence on God." God does not always give us exactly what we want, but he always gives us exactly what we need. From God all good things flow—especially the gift of Jesus and his promise never to leave us.

When we do not get what we want or things do not go our way, we can put up a fight and become callous and angry, *or* we can accept our circumstances, knowing God has a bigger plan. In this way, we take a plunge into the greatest virtue that assists in building humility: gratitude. There is so much to be thankful for, and by humbling ourselves, we can focus on all God has given us, not all the things we wish we had or wish we could do. Every time we thank God and others, we build community and appreciate the people around us, which can ward off any lurking pride in our lives.

Gratefulness comes from understanding our nothingness and recognizing God as the giver of all gifts. If we start anything by saying to ourselves, "I deserve," then we will squelch the power of this great virtue. When we start with the awareness that we are dust and to dust we shall return, then everything that is good is gravy. And sometimes we finally realize Jesus is all we need when he is all we've got. I hope it never has to get to that, which is why gratefulness is imperative.

💡 **QUOTE TO REMEMBER:** "Prayer is an aspiration of the heart, it is a simple glance directed to heaven, it is a cry of gratitude and love in the midst of trial as well as joy." —St. Thérèse of Lisieux

✝ **TIME FOR GOD:** For one whole day, thank God for the great things he has done (don't focus on what you think you lack). If you are really ambitious, do the same with all the people you come in contact with.

🎯 **MAKE IT COUNT:** Take the Love Dare from Ann Voskamp's book *One Thousand Gifts: A Dare to Live Fully Right Where You Are*, and keep a running list of the things you are grateful for. Don't stop until you hit one thousand things. Make sure to have fun with this!

PART V
Be Encouraging

ENTHUSIASM FOR WHAT IS GOOD

Now who is there to harm you if you are zealous for what is right?

—*1 Peter 3:13*

GOOGLY-EYED FOR CHRIST

The road to holiness is not dependent on how battered and used your *Catechism* or Bible is. It is, however, dependent on whether you are in love. Have you ever seen two people who are absolutely head over heels for each other? Have you noticed the way they act as if nothing else in the world matters? They've got "googly eyes" for each other and can't take those eyes off each other. Often they don't seem to be aware that there's a world around them. If we are truly in love with Christ, we should have that same look in our eyes. Two people who are in love get excited about the small things—about anything, as long as they are doing it *with* one another. In our relationship with Christ, are we head over heels like this? Maybe at first we were, but over the years that enthusiasm started to die off, right? When we first started living for Christ, we weren't afraid to get excited about him. We weren't afraid to look a little silly for his sake. But what about now?

The world tells us to be the best, to do it all on our own, to know it all. But Christ tells us to be foolish. Not in a way that is a cop-out in our studies or our work, but in a stepping-out-of-our-comfort-zone way. It's about not being afraid to look like a fool if it means that you fall more in love with God or help another person to experience his love. We need to start getting enthusiastic for Christ!

ENTHUSIASTIC ENCOURAGEMENT

I've heard it said that if you do foolish things but do them with enthusiasm, you're still a winner. I believe that's the story of anyone who wants to help others know how much God loves them. Norman Vincent Peale said that enthusiasm "spells the difference between mediocrity and accomplishment." I believe that if we are enthusiastic for what is truly noble, it will spark change within ourselves and within others. Enthusiasm is an electricity that will help others get through the impossible circumstances that they face in life.

You can change the world with only two simple words. While you're standing in a grocery store line, at a restaurant, at a hardware store, or wherever you like to hang out, look someone in the eyes and genuinely, humbly, prayerfully, and gently say with all your heart, "You're amazing!"—and really mean it. When I do this people will often respond by saying, "Sir, do you know me?" I tell them, "I don't know you, but I know who does." I say this because God knows who they truly are. By saying these two simple words of encouragement, you and I can speak a powerful message to hurting hearts: *You* are amazing, and God believes in you no matter what you've done. You matter!

People tell me they love God, but that they don't need to get excited about him. But when have you loved someone—I mean *really* loved someone—and not been excited about that person? When you love someone, you are naturally enthusiastic about who that person is and what he or she means to you.

I truly believe that Jesus Christ saved my life. If we truly believe this, we will naturally be enthusiastic about it. Many people say that being Catholic is boring. And I think you've probably met some boring Catholics! But if being Catholic is boring, then that means we are boring. Enthusiasm wins most of the time.

QUOTE TO REMEMBER: "The best way to cheer yourself up is to try to cheer somebody else up." —Mark Twain

TIME FOR GOD: Think back to the first time you had a loving encounter with God. How did you talk to him? How did you pray? Ask God what aspects of your relationship with him have been lost, and ask how you can rekindle that early enthusiasm. Look up and pray with Revelation 2:4.

MAKE IT COUNT: Often we waste precious time in our lives that we could be using to grow in our faith. Instead of watching a meaningless sitcom on TV, watch an inspirational YouTube video, and then share the video on your social media pages.

(Some great speakers you can look up are Matthew Kelly, Mark Hart, Bishop Robert Barron, Brian Greenfield, Jason Evert, Fr. Larry Richards, and Christopher West.)

ENJOY YOUR LIFE

*I know that there is nothing better for them than to be
happy and enjoy themselves as long as they live.*

—Ecclesiastes 3:12

BECOMING YOUR AMAZING SELF!

To really enjoy your life, you need to become exactly who God made you to be. For me, this has been a process. Ever since I can remember I've enjoyed speaking in front of people. When I was younger, I was a team mascot called the Erie Otter. I was also a soda pop vendor at a stadium, and everyone called me the Pop Man. I would get the crowds excited about anything and everything. Once I even worked for the New York Mets as a hot dog vendor.

In 1996 my high school class went to see Pope John Paul II in New York City. Our teachers took us on a boat ride to see the Statue of Liberty. Because the pope was there, the boat was full of people. I thought, *This is my opportunity to pick on my teacher, Fr. Larry!* As we were waiting for the boat I soaked up this opportunity. I flipped over a big garbage can and stood right on top of it. I started "preaching," like Fr. Larry. I imitated his burly voice and said, "Hey! Everybody, listen up! Everybody look at me!" Repeating the lesson Fr. Larry always taught us, I said, "You need to love Jesus first! Others second! And yourself last! *That's* how you're going to get joy in life, you pagans! And for all those *atheists* out there, we don't *like* you!" At that point Fr. Larry lost his patience with me, yelling, "*Get off that garbage can!*" That was my first taste of preaching to a whole crowd— little did I know it would become my life's work one day.

Too many of us try to fit into a cookie-cutter image of what we think a Catholic should look like. But God has already cultivated gifts in us that make us amazing. I didn't change my personality when I met Jesus personally. I didn't think, *People who know Jesus are quiet and reverent everywhere they go, so I'd better act like that.* If you were loud and boisterous before Christ, be loud and boisterous with Christ. If you were quiet before Christ, then just be the best listener out there— but with Christ. The only thing that should change after you begin a relationship with God is your sinfulness. Get rid of sin. Everything else—well, that can stay. Don't change who you are, because you're amazing! Once you get rid of your big sins, then focus on growing in virtue to get rid of the rest. But remember that you will never be perfect here on earth. God knows that; he makes allowances for your imperfections, and you should too. Making the most of life means allowing God to interact with our humanness. Rejoice that he loves you for you!

GROW IN YOUR GIFTS

When you are Jesus focused, your life is no longer all about you. When you give your life for others, that is when you are tested and truly find out who you are.

Think about it: You don't enjoy your life when you're doing a million things that you're not good at—you enjoy your life when you hone your gifts. The Gospel says to repent and believe, and when you believe, that is when God grows you. God took the gifts that he gave me from the beginning, and little by little through my walk with him, he's made them greater. He watered the seeds that were planted, and the fruit of my life is only because of that. You have your own, unique set of gifts that God gave you for you and that you could share with the whole world. Stop holding back, and let them rip! We need you and all the amazing self that you are.

QUOTE TO REMEMBER: "The secret of life is enjoying the passage of time." —James Taylor

TIME FOR GOD: Do something you enjoy and turn it into a prayer. Do you paint? Paint for the Lord! Do you play basketball? Play for the Lord! Do you sing? Sing for the Lord!

MAKE IT COUNT: Find someone in your life who is feeling down. Ask him or her to hang out with you, doing his or her favorite activity.

GOD CENTERED, PEOPLE FOCUSED

"And the King will answer them, 'Truly, I say to you, as you did it to one of the least of these my brethren, you did it to me."

—Matthew 25:40

A PICK-ME-UP

One thing that makes our mission unique is our "You're Amazing" bus. It was given to our mission by a generous donor, and as Fr. Peter Cameron says, it's the best sacramental we've got! Our bus enables us to travel from town to town spreading the amazing message of Jesus Christ and the fulfilling life he offers.

When someone boards our bus, we make it our goal to encourage the heck out of him or her. When people check out our bus, we hope it's as if they are meeting Jesus Christ himself. Our goal is to encourage everyone we encounter—not just on the bus, but everywhere—and let them know that they matter. With God at the center of what we do, it's natural that we are people focused— because Jesus was people focused. If we say we love God but we forget about the people around us, then do we really love him? If we love God, we will love and encourage his kids: "If anyone says, 'I love God,' but hates his brother, he is a liar; for whoever does not love a brother whom he has seen cannot love God whom he has not seen. This is the commandment we have from him: whoever loves God must also love his brother" (1 John 4:20–21).

We treat every member of our staff the same way we treat everyone else. Take our bus driver, Mark, for example. Before Mark joined our team, I interviewed him. I asked him, "What's the most challenging time you've ever had in your life?"

"When my wife left me, I was lonely," he told me. Just looking at Mark, you wouldn't imagine how much pain and suffering he went through, because he's always smiling. But I sensed that we needed to encourage him so he could experience the love of God like never before. So we did, and we brought him on board. Now, if you get on the bus, when Mark sees you, he'll tell you, "You're amazing!" You see, when you encourage others, it's contagious—pretty soon they'll start to do the same.

We have to be ready to be God centered and people focused at all times because there are so many suffering souls out there who are wearing masks and saying everything is OK. So many people need a pick-me-up. The "You're Amazing" message is a lot like being a bus driver: They both pick people up!

Jesus wants you and me to believe that we can be that pick-me-up. This doesn't happen every day, but we can do our best to look people in the eye and always be ready to give them the greatest gift on the planet—the gift of letting them know that they matter.

THEY WILL KNOW US BY OUR LOVE

Being God centered means that we act like God. God rescued us from our sin and the penalty of that sin. Now we are here to make known his great mercy and help rescue others. Our goal is that every person we meet may know who God is through our example. If we truly believe that God saved us from sin and death, we won't need to say a word—they will see the hope in our eyes and the love with which we care for others. We are God's hands and feet in this world, so as we interact with others we become the vision of God in that moment for them. As the old saying goes, your life might be the only Gospel someone reads. When you live a life of love, others will know that God is love. It is written all throughout the Bible, but they'll be able to know it by knowing you.

When people see you being gentle, kind, and compassionate, it's the greatest compliment when they think, *If God is anything like this person, then I want to meet that God.* My daughter is the best example of this. I always look to the heavens and say to God, "If you love me half as much as my daughter does, then I'm in!"

QUOTE TO REMEMBER: "Christ has no body on earth but yours, no hands but yours, no feet but yours. Yours are the eyes through which Christ's compassion for the world is to look out; yours are the feet with which he is to go about doing good; and yours are the hands with which he is to bless us now." —St. Teresa of Ávila

TIME FOR GOD: The next time you are hanging out with your friends, focus on their needs, desires, fears, and what's going on in their life, even if you are having a bad day or are in need of encouragement.

MAKE IT COUNT: Encourage a bus driver today. Be a pick-me-up for him as he picks others up. (You can also encourage a train conductor, a restaurant server, a cashier, gas attendant, an Uber driver, an airplane pilot, or anyone your big heart desires.)

DAILY DOSE OF THE WORD OF GOD

For the word of God is living and active, sharper than any two-edged sword, piercing to the division of soul and spirit, of joints and marrow, and discerning the thoughts and intentions of the heart.

—Hebrews 4:12

YOU ARE WHAT YOU . . . READ

I believe reading the Word of God is essential to living a life of fulfillment. We need to learn how amazing we are and the amazing plan God has for our life. The Word of God is the best place to learn what that looks like for each and every one of us. To know Jesus, we need to know his Word. It's helpful to think of the word *Bible* as an acronym: *Basic Instructions Before Leaving Earth.* Most of us do not hear the audible voice of God, and that's why he gave us the Bible—so he can speak to us!

Every day we should open up the Bible and soak up a little of its wisdom. The Book of Wisdom says, "Desire therefore my words; long for them and you shall be instructed. Resplendent and unfading is Wisdom, and she is readily perceived by those who love her, and found by those who seek her" (Wisdom 6:11–12). God is waiting for us to get to know him more, and one guaranteed way to do that is to get in your daily dose of his Word. It's the best medicine in this sick world. Fr. Larry likes to say, "No Bible, no breakfast. No Bible, no bed!"

The Book of Wisdom also calls God the "lover of souls" (Wisdom 11:26), and guess what—the God who loves us wrote each and every one of us a personal letter. Because the Word is "living and effective," as Hebrews 4:12 says, it speaks to everyone in different ways at different times. It can give us all we need, but so often we forget to give it credit. Well, not anymore—dust off that Bible and find out how much you are loved and cared for.

We need to know the Word of God, because when we are discouraged, we can remember his promises to us and remember that with him, we can do all things. We need to memorize the Word so that it becomes a part of our thoughts and actions each day. Our staff has seen the power of the Word in their lives as they memorize verses, and I hear countless stories from my past students at Paramus Catholic High School, in New Jersey, who still cling to verses they memorized for their final exam. God moves in powerful ways when we read, memorize, and take to heart his Word.

A great way to memorize the Word is to find a Bible verse that speaks to you and write it down on a slip of paper. Carry it with you throughout the day, taking it out every once in a while and reading it. Commit it to memory, and share it with a friend or someone in need. I learned this very early on in my walk with God, and it has been a big help. Whenever I ask God to give me a verse to encourage or admonish me, he follows through and helps me to do what he has asked me to do. Just like our parents used to tell us that we are what we eat, we are also what we read. And if we aspire to be like God, the how-to book is right in front of us!

AMAZING VERSES

Our Protestant brothers and sisters get the importance of the Word; hanging out with them definitely helped me to learn the Bible. When I was nineteen years old, I was at a Protestant service where they gave out free Bibles, and I was moved to ask God if one day at our "You're Amazing" events we could give out free Bibles too. It was really just a passing prayer, but God remembered and answered that prayer, and last year on our "You're Amazing" bus tours, we gave away more than sixteen thousand Bibles. We expect this year we'll give out more than fifty thousand.

I believe wholeheartedly that the Word of God is amazing. The more we read it, the more we get to know it, memorize it, use it in our daily lives, and share it with others, the more passionate about our faith we'll become. The Bible is the greatest book in all human history, and not even the English scholars can deny that. Around five billion copies have been printed since 1815—that's pretty impressive! Most important, all forms of encouragement can be summed up in the Word of God. If we fall madly in love with the Word and really listen to God's message, we will not be able to go astray on our path to a fulfilled life.

💡 **QUOTE TO REMEMBER:** "I read novels, but I also read the Bible. And study it, you know? And the more I learn, the more excited I get." —Johnny Cash

✝ **TIME FOR GOD:** Open your Bible and read (particularly in the New Testament, or Psalms or Proverbs) until you reach a verse that hits you. Underline it in your Bible and then write some notes on your phone or in your journal. Make this a daily habit.

🎯 **MAKE IT COUNT:** Get to know the Bible by memorizing these four verses. Get ready to see what a difference it makes in your life.

John 3:16
Romans 8:28
Mark 9:23
John 10:10

THE MOST AMAZING WORDS

For God so loved the world that he gave his only-begotten Son, that whoever believes in him should not perish but have eternal life.

—*John 3:16*

THE "YOU'RE AMAZING" MESSAGE

John 3:16 is the Gospel message of mercy and salvation condensed into one sentence. This Scripture contains the very purpose of life. It has been dear to my heart since I gave my life to Christ in March 1996. It became even more beautiful when my wife, Mary, gave birth to our firstborn son, Joseph. Joseph is ten years old now, and he's scoring touchdowns in flag football and reading two to three books per week. It's incredible how quickly time flies. But when I could hold him in the palm of my hand, John 3:16 blasted me in the heart.

My wife asked me to watch Joseph on my own for the first time just three weeks after he was born. It took her that long to trust me with him by myself because, well, I am not usually the first person people ask to watch their children. As she was heading out the door, she said, "Please make sure you support his neck, if he cries rock him, and don't put him down when he cries."

I received my orders—I was ready to really be a dad for the first time. This was when the "You're Amazing" message became real in my life. Up until that point, I had always thought my success was measured by what I achieved. Failure was not an option. I had pressure and I had purpose, measured only by my deeds.

Then the door slammed. Mary was leaving. It was time to realize how amazing I truly was. A few minutes went by and it felt exhilarating to be a dad. But soon enough, three-week-old Joseph started to screech. It was as though someone was yelling at him and he was screaming back in fear. Growing up, I was the youngest child in my family, with a brother four years older and a sister eleven years older than I was, so I hadn't had many encounters with screaming babies. Needless to say, this was a new experience—my first wild encounter with a newborn. So the preacher deep within me surfaced, and I did the only thing I knew to do. It was time to encourage my newborn. I dug deep inside and told him, "You're amazing! You're the best! You matter to me!"

I thought back to when my wife went through labor, the most excruciating pain that I have ever seen anyone experience, and how she showed love for another human like I had never witnessed before. She endured thirty-six hours of intense labor pains in order to bring Joseph into the world. It reminded me in a small way of when Our Lady was at the foot of the cross watching her Son die. As she saw Jesus experiencing intense pain, she must have questioned why it had to happen. I imagined my wife saying the same to God the Father: "Why?" It was the first time I looked up at God and thought, *You created this labor experience? Man, you are a sicko.* (Forgive me, God, but I'm just being real.)

After thirty-six hours of labor, Joseph came down the slip-and-slide into the world. My thoughts changed to *WOW! Women are amazing!* Joseph changed my life.

Now, three weeks later, I looked at him, crying his little lungs out, and I said, "I am so proud of you, son." It didn't matter what he did; it was about who he was. As Joseph was crying while I held him, I told him, "I am proud of you, son, even if you cry." He looked at me as people do when they are sizing someone up, wondering what this person's deal is. He just stared at me. I said again, "I am proud of you, even if you're staring at me! No matter how you look, I am proud of you!"

While I was busy talking, I got distracted and forgot about his neck. I was holding him up, but without support, his neck was wobbling back and forth and I thought, *Oh no, his neck might break. Mary told me to watch his neck!* Suddenly it all connected—John 3:16 became more real and more beautiful than I could have imagined. I supported my son's neck and said, "I am proud of you, son. I am proud of you whether you get As or Fs in school. I am proud of you even if you make mistakes. There is nothing that can make me not proud of you."

GOD IS SO PROUD OF YOU

Then God really grabbed my attention. The most powerful moments in life are often when people fight through pain to get to joy. Sometimes pain is a warning sign, and at other times, it's needed to get us to do what God wants us to do. God works through our pain to teach us to depend on him. If you never had a problem, you'd never get to see how God could solve it. I realize that you don't know that God is all you need until God is all you have. Paul said it well in 2 Corinthians 1:6: "If we are afflicted, it is for your encouragement and salvation; if we are encouraged, it is for your encouragement, which enables you to endure the same sufferings that we suffer."

Holding my little son, I had tears running down my face, like a faucet that just wouldn't stop. I finally understood the true meaning of the cross. The most encouraging message in all of human history is that God sent Jesus to go through all that pain and suffering to ultimately give me the greatest joy. God loves me. He is so proud of me that he sent his only Son to endure a bloody death *to set me free*. This instant of sheer love and respect for my son led me to this aha moment of fulfillment that I struggle even now to put into words (so bear with me).

What hit me so hard was that the great love I felt for Joseph was so small in comparison to the love that God, the King of the Universe, feels for me and for all of us. No matter what we do, God would still give everything, and he has—he still freely sent Jesus to save us. At times in life I think I am not good enough, but at that magnificent moment, I realized that Jesus was enough for me and for all of us. It's OK that I'm not perfect, because if I were, then I wouldn't need a savior.

God is so proud of me, I thought, but what about everyone else? What about those who have been abused or injured at the hands of others, the sick, the lonely, the poor and the homeless, or even those who have been injured at their own hands? Many people focus on John 3:16 and forget what John 3:17 says: "For God did not send his Son into the world to condemn the world, but that the world might be saved through him." God's most impressive achievement is sending his Son to this world for you and me at no cost to us. No matter who we are or what we have done, God sent Jesus Christ to save us from our own sinfulness. That is the message of mercy. Jesus takes what is due us. It's not about what I do or don't do; instead, it's about who I am—and I am a child of God. I'm in his family and he is proud of me. And God is proud of *you*.

Isn't that powerful? Isn't that *amazing*?

QUOTE TO REMEMBER: "Sin's masterpiece of shame and hate became God's masterpiece of mercy and forgiveness. Through the death of Christ upon the cross, sin itself was crucified for those who believe in Him." —Billy Graham

TIME FOR GOD: Take one minute, and with every beat of your heart, picture God saying to you, "I am proud of you, son [or daughter]; that is why I sent my Son for you."

MAKE IT COUNT: Today tell someone you love just how proud God is of him or her. When we encourage others with the truth that God loves them, it is much more powerful than if we encourage them with only our own words.

EXPECT THE BEST

Therefore I tell you, all that you ask for in prayer,
believe that you will receive it and it shall be yours.

—*Mark 11:24*

We all have bad days occasionally. If we expect God to make our day better, nine times out of ten, we will see him moving in a little way. But if we expect our day to go badly, I believe we will miss all the opportunities for God to show his majestic power even amid horrible circumstances. So let's expect the best and let God do the rest.

RECEIVE WHAT YOU BELIEVE

You aren't fulfilled because you don't expect to be. Scripture tells us that what you believe is what you receive. Romans 10:9 says, "If you confess with your mouth that Jesus is Lord and *believe in your heart* that God raised him from the dead, you will be saved." If you believe that God has called you to greatness and has set you on a path to fulfillment, you are halfway there. What we allow to enter our minds will eventually form our hearts; what we believe in our hearts is what will come to fruition in our lives. We need to begin today to put plans of fulfillment in our minds so that our hearts will be transformed. Once our hearts are formed, we will be able to expect the best, just like Christ, and truly begin a life of fulfillment.

JESUS WAS AN OPTIMIST

Basic psychology tells us that our thought patterns, both positive and negative, affect the way we live our lives and the way we view the world around us. When we have a positive attitude, we are able to see the good in all situations. But when we are "negative Nancys," even the smallest inconveniences in life seem to beat us down. If we were to do an experiment on an optimistic person versus a pessimistic person by putting them both in three hours of traffic on a Friday afternoon, the results would be quite interesting. An optimist would focus on the beautiful view of the clouds overhead, listen to the radio, and enjoy feeling the wind between his fingers as he dangled his arm out the window. On the other hand, the pessimist might be grunting, cursing, and white-knuckled at the thought of how long she might be stuck behind this . . . cough, cough . . . *amazing* person who just cut her off.

So which person is living a life of fulfillment? Grunting and cursing might be satisfying for the pessimist in the moment, but accepting the inconvenience in front of you with joy will give you inner peace. Living a life of fulfillment doesn't mean having a perfect life; it means making the best out of life even when it gets frustrating, ugly, or even painful.

Jesus lived a fulfilling life—he was an optimist. He never despaired, even at his darkest hour. During the agony in the garden, he went through the most excruciating mental, spiritual, and emotional pain that a human has ever endured, yet he accepted what his Father had planned for him: "My Father, if it is possible, let this cup pass from me; yet, not as I will, but as you will" (Matthew 26:39). Jesus trusted that God knew what was best for him, and we must do the same. Do you trust God?

QUOTE TO REMEMBER: "Expect the best, plan for the worst, and prepare to be surprised." —Unknown

TIME FOR GOD: For a week straight, pray for a person in your life whom you dread seeing. Next time you see that person, say a prayer to be able to see him or her as God does. Expect God to come through in amazing ways.

MAKE IT COUNT: Use the notes app on your phone, or write out in your journal this verse: "For God so loved _____ (place your name here) that he gave _____ his only Son, so that if _____ believes in him _____ might not perish but might have eternal life." (John 3:16)

Write out one Bible verse every day for ninety days and see if it makes a difference in your life.

ENDURANCE INSPIRES

But the one who endures to the end will be saved.

—Matthew 24:13

The greatest way to encourage others is to endure your trials with a smile. Recently some friends of mine told me that they'd had a son who had died and how badly it had hurt them. But then, they smiled and told me how much it had taught them. I just sat there, awestruck, and thought, *If one of my sons died, I'd be a complete mess!* Does that mean it was easy for them to go through such a loss? No. It means that people can be an encouragement to others by enduring faithfully, hopefully, and triumphantly the battles life throws their way. If my friends had given up when it got tough, I'd be so discouraged. But seeing them persevere gets me fired up to keep going.

LIFE ISN'T EASY

The divorce rate continues to skyrocket. A leading cause of death in the United States is suicide. Millions of women have experienced an attempted rape or a completed rape. People all around us are hurting and struggling. The best way we can lift them up is by persevering through our own challenges in the power of Christ. How do we handle confrontation? How do *we* handle tragedy? Do we close the door and simply give up? Or do we endure in a way that brings hope to a hurting world? I believe that the greatest way to motivate, encourage, inspire, and uplift others is to let them know that we've experienced many of life's challenges too—and instead of allowing them to cause frenzy in our lives, we've been able to learn and grow from them; they've made us into the men and women we are today.

One of my friends almost died earlier this year. She was pregnant and the doctors told her not to go through with the birth because of complications, but she did—and survived. Another one of my good friends, a thirty-one-year-old football star, was diagnosed with bone cancer. He had to fight through eighteen rounds of chemo and now walks with a cane. These friends do not discourage me because of the suffering they've been through, though. They give me the courage to say to myself, "I could never go through what they've been through. They are my heroes! Because of their example I can face my own challenges with trust and hope."

One of my favorite characters of all time is Rocky Balboa, the main character in the *Rocky* movies. He said, "It's not about how hard you get hit; it's about how hard you can get hit and keep moving forward. . . . That's how winning is done." Endurance is about inspiring others to win regardless of situations that seem designed to bring them down and cause them to give up when the going gets tough. When we allow ourselves to give up, it's a sign that we have lost confidence in Christ, who is always ready to give us the strength and power to endure suffering.

BLESSED ARE THE HOMELESS AND HOMEBOUND

Do you look at someone in a wheelchair and say, "Wow, that person inspires me!" rather than feeling sorry for him or her? Or when you see a homeless person begging for money, do you see that person's life as a mess and say to yourself, "Don't get too close—you don't know if you can trust people like that"? When we live a life of fulfillment, we can see them as amazing. God has created each of us to be amazing, no matter what.

When I see homeless people on the street, I'll go up to them and thank them. They will look at me like I have four heads. Then I'll say, "I impact thousands of people all over the world by preaching the Gospel, but you will impact more people than I ever could—every day!" When they look at me, they might think, *Who is this guy and what is his deal?* But when I talk to them, encourage them, and show them that I really care about them, they listen. Maybe they were feeling hopeless that day, but a simple word of encouragement can put somebody back on track for days or weeks.

The homeless inspire others because although they have endured various trials and are still on the streets, they haven't given up. They show up for something simple, maybe just a cup of coffee, but their impact is great. We need to start looking at those who have gone through difficult trials in life as heroes and not as a disease. These heroes may be counted as nothing to most of the world, but we have a lot to learn from their endurance. We need to be like the homeless who never gave up, and be people who will inspire others by enduring until the end.

QUOTE TO REMEMBER: "Endurance is not just the ability to bear a hard thing, but to turn it into glory." —William Barclay

TIME FOR GOD: Ask God, "Who in my life has lost hope?" Give that person a phone call today and encourage him or her not to give up.

MAKE IT COUNT: Ask yourself these two questions and then listen to your heart:

1. What have I given up on?
2. Whom have I given up on?

Then make a commitment to start over and learn to endure. Fulfillment comes when you start fresh and never give up.

THE GREATEST LIFE EVER

[Jesus] is before all things, and in him all things hold
together. He is the head of the body, the Church; he is the
beginning, the first-born from the dead, that in every-
thing he might be pre-eminent. For in him all the fullness
of God was pleased to dwell, and through him to reconcile
to himself all things, whether on earth or in heaven,
making peace by the blood of his cross.

—Colossians 1:17–20

I'm hoping you picked up this book because the promise of a life
of fulfillment appeals to you—and that you would like to help
others find an amazing life too. Maybe this book was given to
you, or maybe you picked it up at your church, or maybe you
even found it at a garage sale. But it's not about *how* you picked
it up, it's about *why* you picked it up. And *why* you picked it up
is to find out who you truly are. As we have learned, when you

find out how amazing you are with Jesus, you will help others to see the same in themselves. With Jesus, you will be inspiring. You, my friend, have power—more power than you know. You are a witness and encouragement for others, and *who* you are matters!

If all of us lived the abundant life Jesus promised, our churches would be packed. Most people come to the church looking for evidence of the greatest life ever lived, but often they come out empty-handed. People of the world are looking for you to give them hope that this exists. They are hungry for an example of Jesus Christ's love. You can be that example. You can help others realize that a life of fulfillment is possible with Jesus, because when you get through trials they will see that it is only the hope of glorious fulfillment that gets you through. When people see that you are fulfilled, they will want what you have. They will desire the way, the truth, and the life because of you, because they have seen you suffer well and still experience fulfillment. At times, your hope and joy will be so full it will overflow in abundance; at other times, you will be low and need help from a friend. Be that friend first, and give until it hurts. Then and only then will your reward be great in heaven.

People think they have it all. The American dream is dangerous, and it is letting people down daily. They have cars, money, and smartphones, but they're going to sleep at night lonely, discouraged, and in disarray. They might have money and fame, but it comes with a lot of emptiness and pain. They need to know they are amazing. They need to know it's possible live a life of fulfillment. You might be just the encouragement they need to fulfill their dreams, their hopes, and their future. Our mission in life should be to let the whole world know that they are amazing. We are all amazing because God made us and he is proud of us.

YOU ARE UNSTOPPABLE

At the end of the year, I always ask our missionaries this question: What is one thing you learned from your formation, your time in the office, and your time traveling with us across the nation to impact thousands of people? Their answers always vary, but one always sticks out in my mind, and I think it applies to us here today. With a heart of gold and a quiet but strong, sweet little voice of conviction, humility, and passion, one nineteen-year-old missionary raised her hand, looked me in the eye, and said, "I learned that I am *unstoppable*." And you'd better believe you are too. If you carry out the five ways to live a life of fulfillment outlined in this book, you will be a force to be reckoned with. A life of fulfillment is a life of purpose and hope that will transform you forever. Pope Benedict XVI once said, "You were not made for comfort. You were made for greatness." And it's true. Living a life of fulfillment will not be comfortable, nor will it be easy—*nothing* great comes easy. But it will set you up with the greatest life ever.

Our missionaries come each year to serve, but they quickly find out that in giving, they receive, and what they receive most of all is a clearer picture of their amazing selves. The day you realize that anything is possible with God is the day you realize just how unstoppable you are. Stop fighting, and live the greatest life ever. When you surrender you will be given that new heart and new life you have been looking for. And then, when you have found it deep within, share your life of fulfillment with everyone you meet. One day you will die, and so will I. And then, I can't wait to see you in heaven, where every desire of ours will be filled to overflowing! I don't say good-bye, so I'll leave you with how I say farewell to everyone I meet: "If I don't see you, I'll see you in heaven!"

QUOTE TO REMEMBER: "The pinnacle of the fulfillment I can ever experience for my spirit and soul is to hear from the Lord, when I see him face to face, 'Well done my good and faithful servant.'" —Nick Vujicic

TIME FOR GOD: Go to your local church and spend an hour in silence before Jesus. Ask him what lessons he wants you to take with you from this book.

MAKE IT COUNT: Share this book with someone who you know is looking for more in life. Don't keep this life of fulfillment to yourself—pass it on to those you care about. Let them know that they are amazing and that you believe in them!

ACKNOWLEDGMENTS

I would like to dedicate this book to my wife, Mary, who is an exceptional mother and an example of God's love to all she meets. Go Team Fatica!

I would also like to thank all those who helped make this book possible: The Beacon Publishing team, Matthew Kelly, Claudia Volkman, Kristen Whalen, and our wonderful team at Hard as Nails (rememberyoureamazing.com), the missionaries and staff who are dedicated to bringing the "You're Amazing" message to everyone they meet.

A special thank-you to Morgan Agia and Teresa Liguori who have generously poured themselves into this project. They have helped make this book a powerful spiritual resource for anyone who wants to live the Gospel message. They are both exemplary missionaries and examples of what it means to live out their baptismal calling. They are amazing!

Thank you for all your hard work and determination. I hope this book is a gift that will change the world in dynamic ways.

HAVE YOU EVER
WONDERED HOW THE
CATHOLIC FAITH
COULD HELP YOU
LIVE BETTER?

How it could help you find more *joy* at work, *manage* your personal finances, *improve* your marriage, or make you a *better* parent?

THERE IS GENIUS IN CATHOLICISM.

When *Catholicism* is lived as it is intended to be, it elevates every part of our lives. It may sound simple, but they say *genius is taking something complex and making it simple.*

Dynamic Catholic started with a dream: to help ordinary people discover the *genius of Catholicism.*

Wherever you are in your journey, we want to meet you there and walk with you, *step by step*, helping you to discover God and become *the-best-version-of-yourself.*

To find more helpful resources, visit us
online at DynamicCatholic.com.

 Dynamic Catholic